One of the least known aspects of Stubbs' work was his work on ceramic. This originally sprang from his co-operation with Josiah Wedgwood, whom he contacted in 1775, enquiring whether the master-potter could provide him with ceramic plaques for 'canvases'.

Written to accompany an exhibition at the Tate Gallery and published on the 250th anniversary of Stubbs' birth, this book illustrates and discusses more than thirty works related to the Wedgwood connection. Stubbs' investigation into the use of enamel colour before he met Wedgwood is also dealt with and there are a number of extracts from Wedgwood's letters concerning the artist.

The author, Bruce Tattersall, is Curator of the Wedgwood Museum at Barlaston. Basil Taylor, authority and author of a recent book on the life and work of Stubbs, has contributed an introduction.

Stubbs & Wedgwood

BRUCE TATTERSALL

STUBBS & WEDGWOOD

Unique alliance
between Artist and Potter

with an introduction by BASIL TAYLOR

THE TATE GALLERY

Exclusively distributed in France and Italy by Idea Books
24 rue du 4 Septembre, Paris (2e) and Via Cappuccio 21, 20123 Milan

ISBN 0 900874 80 5 paper 0 900874 81 3 cloth
Published by order of the Trustees 1974
for the exhibition of 19 June – 18 August 1974
Copyright © 1974 The Tate Gallery
Designed and published by the Tate Gallery Publications Department,
Millbank, London SW1P 4RG
Printed in Great Britain by The Hillingdon Press, Uxbridge

Contents

Cover illustration
The Frightened Horse (detail)
Catalogue No. 23 c

Foreword

1974 is the 250th anniversary of the birth of George Stubbs and it is, I think, therefore fitting that it should see an exhibition devoted to one of the most under-estimated facets of the artist's work – his paintings in enamel on Wedgwood plaques.

The association between George Stubbs and Josiah Wedgwood was a unique alliance of artist and industrialist and the aim of the exhibition is to show the fruits of their labours in this field both individually and together. Particularly pleasing are the works which Wedgwood commissioned from Stubbs which are brought together for the first time since 1796.

We are grateful to the Wedgwood Directors and the Museum Trustees for their co-operation and assistance in presenting the exhibition and in particular to both Bruce Tattersall, curator of the Wedgwood Museum, who has selected the exhibits and written the catalogue, and to Basil Taylor who has very kindly written an introduction. We are also grateful to all the lenders who have made the exhibition possible.

Norman Reid, *Director, The Tate Gallery*

Preface

The Directors of Wedgwood and the Trustees of the Wedgwood Museum are pleased to be associated with the Tate Gallery in this exhibition.

The co-operation between Wedgwood and Stubbs was a signal example of how well the arts and science can combine in a venture which was a *tour de force* for both protagonists. Wedgwood with his characteristic energy threw himself into an enterprise in which other potters would have lacked the abilities and resources to make an effective contribution. The company has always been proud of this association, and works modelled by Stubbs have been frequently produced since the artist's visit to Etruria in 1780.

I am pleased that the results can be seen in this monograph and exhibition demonstrating the union of arts and industry – a tradition we strive to maintain today.

Arthur Bryan, *Chairman, Josiah Wedgwood & Sons Ltd*

Stubbs and the Art of Painted Enamel

The following notes are intended to provide a view of this exhibition's theme from the standpoint of a student of Stubbs's career as a whole so as to reinforce the presentation here of his relationship with Josiah Wedgwood.

Stubbs's work in enamel colours was certainly the most uncommon and unpredictable undertaking of a very independent artist, as well as being that which raises the widest range of obdurate historical and artistic problems. Those connected to matters of technique may partly be answered by research, but the questions relating to motive, purpose and artistic decision can only be approached speculatively because, in relation to them, there is almost no firm, unambiguous evidence. Here, as elsewhere in the study of the painter's work, we have to examine the pictorial evidence without much explicit guidance from verbal documents or even contemporary reports, and the main excuse for speculation is that thereby we may at least bring into focus the conditions and choices which faced the artist at the time.

Why, to take the most appealing and significant question first, did Stubbs decide to use a material that no other painter of comparable talent has employed, not only in the 18th century but at any time, and why so at a point in his career, at some time in the late seventeen-sixties, when, as a painter in oil colours, his reputation and material success were both, apparently, at their zenith? In the short period since he had established his practice in London at the beginning of the decade Stubbs had gained a commanding reputation among those who were painting animals, the life of the countryside and the recreations associated therewith. In the years around 1770 he was evidently seeking to accommodate his work to artistic aspirations which, although by no means new in English art, were being intensified by the creation of the Royal Academy and the activity of Reynolds, its ambitious President and the most influential artistic ideologist of the time. In Stubbs' case this meant trying to extend the range of his subjects into the sphere of history and beyond what he had already attempted earlier there in treating a theme especially appropriate to an animal painter, 'Phaeton' (16, 17, 18); it was in 1770 and 1772 that he exhibited two of his few other history works, 'Hercules and Achelous' and 'Nessus and Dejanira', both since lost.

It seems unlikely that he was attempting to connect the interpretation of the themes with the use of enamel colours, but at least he did use the material chiefly for subjects which would establish him finally as a painter of something more than horses, dogs and the field sports, and small scale, informal portraits. The enamel paintings on copper dated between 1769 and 1775 include one history piece (another version of Phaeton), two pictures best described as

'Fancy' pieces ('Hope Nursing Love' (7)) and a ('Mother and Child' (6)), and several of those compositions which introduced a dramatic element into animal painting, especially new versions of a favoured theme, a lion frightening or assaulting a wild horse. Simply, we do not know why Stubbs began to use enamels or why, with Wedgwood's assistance, he continued to do so.

If Stubbs was merely seeking to introduce novelty into his practice with the hope of reinforcing his reputation thereby, then it was not the material which was new, even the essential manner of using it, but its employment by someone with his artistic identity and status. Painted enamels had previously occurred in the embellishment of small objects, useful and decorative – snuff boxes, scent bottles and other containers as well as bijouteries and decorative 'toys' – and in the execution of miniature portraits. (Cosway, who is reported by Humphry to have put the idea into Stubbs' mind, probably worked in both these spheres). Indeed a great number of enamelled objects, including some slight, small pictures, had been made in England during the past decades, for example at Jansson's Battersea factory between 1753 and 1756, and in the Midland work-shops at Bilston, Wednesbury, Birmingham and elsewhere. Stubbs' products were in most significant respects different from these: whereas they were produced by skilled, sometimes sophisticated, craftsmen working to satisfy the taste for Rococo ornament and themes and for other prevailing modes in design, whereas they were, in form and subject, reproductive or derivative. Stubbs was a painter of high, if not the highest, repute, making pictures to the limits of his inventiveness and skill and according to the dictates of his own distinctive vision. Where and from whom he learnt the craft, in what kilns his enamels were fired, whether he painted his compositions on to surfaces – copper plates furnished with a white enamel flux – prepared for him by others or whether he made these himself, are facts unlikely to be discovered. Even the preparation of the colours that he used cannot be understood with certainty. Humphry's report that he succeeded in isolating nineteen distinct colours can bear several inter-pretations. At one unlikely extreme it could be taken that he deliberately neglected the standing traditions of the craft and set out from scratch by his own experiments to obtain the particular range of pigments his art demanded. It seems equally improbable that a man of his empirical outlook would have simply adopted or adapted the materials and recipes hitherto used by others.

We may be sure however, that the second phase of the enterprise, which must as Mr Tattersall indicates have begun before 1775, was occasioned by the limitations of working on a copper base.

The association with Wedgwood affords a little more evidence about matters of technique than is available for the earlier period, but even that information is limited and sometimes not very specific. The extent to which the potter may have contributed, if at all, to the painter's development of his pigments cannot be established, but it is obvious that the two men would have had a common professional interest in such a problem. It seems likely that Wedgwood kilns, both at Etruria and in London, were used for firing the works, but there is no indication where any particular work was thus completed. There is also no evidence by which to determine whether by some date, say before 1782, Stubbs had acquired from his collaborator a sufficient stock of tablets to meet his future requirements. Even the difference between the physical attributes of the works on copper and those on a ceramic base give questions currently unanswerable. The earlier pieces have a quality of surface similar to Battersea enamels, for example, but the Wedgwood pieces are to a degree more painterly, showing a slightly greater density of pigment and a distinct, less glassy, finish. The differences in execution, contingent upon the difference and nature of the two supports, must have had some influence upon this change, but may also reflect the artist's wish to give the larger pictures an identity more compatible with paintings in oil colours. It is quite evident, however, that Stubbs's technique in that medium was significantly affected by his practice in enamels, for after 1770 he began frequently to use panels rather than canvas, these providing a surface closely akin to that upon which he was working in the other material, and the depth of his impasto in oils was noticeably less than what had been customary in the seventeen-sixties.

The first extant works painted on ceramic tablets show the artist persisting with at least one type of subject previously treated on the copper base, that is pictures of wild animals. The most important new departure was the creation of portraits, but our interpretation of this development has to be influenced by the fact that with few exceptions the works painted before 1782 were either commissioned or never sold. For Josiah Wedgwood Stubbs painted portraits of him and of his wife (9, 10) and the enamel version of the 'Labourers' (11). The portraits of Isabella Saltonstall (25), Mr Huth (24) and Mr Walker were probably commissioned by the sitters or in the case of the first of these, by a relative. The painter made the half-length portrait (B) of himself for an existing patron. The pictures of two stallions fighting (D) and the equestrian self-portrait (F) were both in his possession at his death.

Once again we are faced by the question whether there was a significant connection between his ambition – admitted to Wedgwood – to be considered as a portrait painter and his practice in enamel colours. I do not believe that Wedgwood's remark that 'the exhibition may do wonders for him' should be understood as meaning the exhibition of works in enamel specifically, for it is more likely that the words apply simply to the Royal Academy exhibition in general, Stubbs having been elected an associate member of that institution a few months before Wedgwood wrote the relevant letter to Bentley. Whether or not this interpretation is correct, the showing of the enamels there was not to be a success and the Academy's way of hanging them, objectionable to the painter, seems to have been one element in the dispute connected with his failure to assume full membership.

There seems to have been a long gap in the production of enamels between 1782 and 1791, when he painted the portrait of Warren Hastings (F), for there is no evidence indicating that he continued to work in the medium during these eight or nine years. And as there is almost no documentary evidence either relating to Stubbs' life and affairs in general during this time, the hiatus cannot be explained. There is only, for these years, a body of dated or datable pictures, including the fifteen mezzotints published between 1788 and 1791. There is no reason in fact to suppose that in this period he was involved in further technical research and experiment comparable with the activities of the seventeen-seventies. The only significant difference between the enamels produced around 1780 and those painted after 1790 – three farming subjects as well as the Hastings portrait – is a certain lightening in the general tone of the compositions and a strengthening of the colour, qualities also to be found in the oil paintings of the same period. It is clear also that he did not take up enamel painting again with any strong intention of trying to persuade patrons and contemporary opinion to accept these things. The Hastings portrait was not exhibited at the Academy in 1791 and he did not exhibit at all there in the years 1792 to 1798. The three farming subjects (G, H, I), dated 1794 and 1795, were all in the studio at his death.

The existing contemporary comments upon the enamels show that they were not well received but, 18th century art reviewing being as undeveloped and unsophisticated as it was, there is no reasoned and substantial argument against them to be found. We can only speculate once again about the reasons for their failure and unpopularity.

To regard the best of the enamels – and some of them are necessarily absent from the present exhibition – as being inferior to Stubbs's similar compositions in oil colours is to neglect qualities, beauties, refinements indeed which they possess *sui generis*. That achievement is more important than the undoubted fact, useful today, that because Stubbs was able to exercise so great a control of his demanding medium, we can discover in them qualities of colour and tone, undiminished by time, which in so many of the oil paintings have been expelled by clumsy cleaning and restoration.

By contrast with cloisonné, champlevé and basse-taille enamels, which can all be treated as quite distinct and independent forms of pictorial art, painted enamels, that technique which Stubbs employed and one with which the name Limoges is most often associated, can rightly be regarded as a form of reproductive art. I suspect that some of the artist's contemporaries regarded his enamel painting as being both a laborious effort of reproduction and as a quixotic, unreasoning attempt to dignify a humble craft. It would however be wrong to treat these works as being reproductive and nothing more than that in spite of the fact that some of them repeated subjects expressed in another medium, as wrong indeed as it would be to regard his mezzotints as nothing but reproductive engravings. The latter so far extended and exploited the resources of mezzotint as to result in works which also possess the personal qualities we associate with the terms 'painter-engraver' and 'artist-print'. In using enamel, Stubbs took a medium hitherto employed in England for modest, indeed trivial exercises and gave it not only a quite unpredictable scale but also as much eloquence and expressiveness as he could command. These works are certainly a sign, if not wholly a product, of his serious and experimental curiosity. That they are also the product not only of an intense relationship with the visible world, like the rest of his painting, but of a contest with the mysteries of chemistry and the hardly biddable force of fire gives them their unique fascination and particularity among the works of the 18th century.

Introduction

This exhibition grew out of several happy coincidences. The first was my conversation with Mr Allan Smith of the University of Manchester as to whether the Stubbs enamels in the Lady Lever Art Gallery were fired or not. The second was my appointment as Curator of the Wedgwood Museum, which put into my charge some of the most interesting and best documented works by the artist, giving me an unrivalled opportunity to examine the Wedgwood archives for information on the alliance between Stubbs and Wedgwood. The final coincidence was the 250th anniversary of Stubbs' birth and the generosity of the Trustees of the Tate Gallery in mounting an exhibition which would not only celebrate this event, but also commemorate his partnership with Wedgwood.

The ideal of this exhibition was to assemble in one place all the known works by Stubbs in enamel, both on copper and Wedgwood plaques, accompanied by the works Stubbs executed for Wedgwood on his visit to Etruria in 1780. Unfortunately ideals are seldom realised and for many reasons, above all the fragile nature of the earthenware plaques, this exhibition can only show a representative selection.

It has, however, still succeeded in the aim of showing that there is a continuum between the enamels on both copper and ceramic and that, from the subjects he chose to portray in enamel, it can be seen that Stubbs himself considered such works just as valid, artistically, as those in more orthodox media. It is hoped that this exhibition will lead to an aesthetic reappraisal of these underestimated paintings.

I hope that in demonstrating the prominent part which Wedgwood played in the enterprise – his independent interest in enamel painting; his constant experimenting – the exhibition will show that he was far more than Stubbs' 'canvas maker'. The making, firing, and re-firing of the plaques was no mean feat in itself.

Particularly happy is the assembly of all the works which Stubbs painted for Etruria Hall. Four of these: the family portrait and those of Richard, Sarah and Josiah Wedgwood belong to the Wedgwood Museum; but the fifth, the 'Labourers', is in a private collection and it is through the generosity of its anonymous owner that we can see these paintings together for the first time since 1796.

My thanks and acknowledgements are many and profound; to the Trustees and staff of the Tate Gallery my thanks for approving the exhibition and for the transfer of certain works from their collections for the exhibition; to the Trustees of the Wedgwood Museum, Barlaston, and Josiah Wedgwood & Sons Limited for loaning the essential works from their museum; also to all the other generous institutions who have loaned works to the exhibition.

Many people have advised and assisted me in my work, special thanks to

Ralph Fastnedge, Professor Michael Jaffé and the staff of the Fitzwilliam Museum, Cambridge, the staff of the Picton Library, Liverpool, to Timothy Clifford of the Victoria and Albert Museum for advice on 'young Stringer', to Iain Fraser, the archivist at Keele University.

I must also express my thanks to Mr Basil Taylor who is the *fons et origino* of Stubbs scholarship.

Bruce Tattersall

Sources and Bibliography

The principal source for letters and documents relating to the relationship between Stubbs and Wedgwood is the Wedgwood Archive, which is currently being transferred from the Wedgwood factory to the University of Keele. For these papers there are two series: the Etruria papers and the Leith Hill Place papers. The Etruria papers are catalogued with a double series number prefixed by an E, viz. E.25.18791. The Leith Hill Place accumulation is uncatalogued and referred to as L.H.P. Most of the documents cited are from Wedgwood to his partner Thomas Bentley and are signified thus: J.W. to T.B.

The other important accumulation is that which belonged to Joseph Mayer, the Liverpool antiquarian and collector. These papers are deposited in the Liverpool Public Library and are referred to as the Mayer papers. Here the most important individual document is the unpublished manuscript biography of Stubbs written from his own recollections by his friend and fellow artist, Ozias Humphry.

All quotations and titles are given with their original spelling and phraseology.

Sale Catalogues

Two sale catalogues are most important for the study of this subject, these are:

1. *The Catalogue of all the remaining Valuable Collection of Original Paintings the Property and Performance of that ingenious and celebrated British Artist, George Stubbs Esq., Dec. . . .* Peter Coxe, 26, 27 May 1807, 24 Somerset Street, London. Referred to as the 1807 sale. Victoria and Albert Museum Library.

2. *Catalogue of the Collection of Sporting Pictures and Works by George Morland of the Late Sir Walter Gilbey, Bart.* Messrs Christie, Manson & Woods, Elsenham Hall, 11 June 1915. By courtesy of Messrs Christie, Manson & Woods; annotated copy in their possession.

Bibliography (all reference in the catalogue to these works is by surname)

Mayer, Joseph, *Early Exhibitions of Art in Liverpool with some Notes for a memoir of George Stubbs R.A.*, privately printed, Liverpool, 1876.

Gilbey, Sir Walter, Bart., *Life of George Stubbs R.A.*, privately printed, London, 1896.

Farrer, Lady Euphemia, *The Letters of Josiah Wedgwood*, privately printed, London, 1903–9; reprinted, Eric Morten in association with the Wedgwood Museum, Barlaston, 1974.

Williamson, G. C., *The Imperial Russian Dinner Service*, London, 1909.
Liverpool, Walker Art Gallery, *George Stubbs 1724–1806*, catalogue, 1951.
Whitechapel Art Gallery, *George Stubbs 1724–1806*, catalogue, 1957.
McKendrick, 'Josiah Wedgwood and George Stubbs', *History Today*, April 1957.

Taylor, Basil (1), 'Josiah Wedgwood and George Stubbs', *Proceedings of the Wedgwood Society*, No. 4, 1961.

Finer, Anne and Savage, George, *The Selected Letters of Josiah Wedgwood*, London, 1965.

Taylor, Basil (2), 'George Stubbs: "The Lion and Horse" theme', *Burlington Magazine*, CVII, 1965.

Taylor, Basil (3), *The Prints of George Stubbs*, London, the Paul Mellon Foundation, 1969.

Taylor, Basil (4), *Stubbs*, Phaidon Press, London, 1971.

Parker, Constance-Anne, *Mr Stubbs the Horse Painter*, J. & A. Allan & Co. Ltd, London, 1971.

Stubbs and Wedgwood

George Stubbs was born in Liverpool in 1724 and Josiah Wedgwood in Burslem in The Potteries in 1730. Apart from being close contemporaries they both possessed that spirit of dispassionate scientific enquiry which emerged in so many of their generation. Until their first contact, in about 1775,[1] they individually followed their careers in a way which firmly united the arts and sciences.

Wedgwood, the Master Potter, developed the fine ceramic bodies called Queen's Ware, Basalt and Jasper by dint of continuous methodical experimentation over some forty years. This scientific *savoir-faire* was combined with an artistic appreciation and business acumen which made his products world-famous.

Stubbs had pursued not only his painting career but also had produced a most important anatomical work *Anatomy of the Horse* published in 1766, which involved him in the single-handed dissection of carcasses, detailed scientific drawings and the engraving of copper plates.

Before 1770[2] Stubbs' scientific curiosity led him to the study of painting in enamel colours. A friend and fellow artist, Richard Cosway, who indulged in a profitable side-line in erotic enamels, assisted this interest, leading to Stubbs' researches into colours which would remain true after firing.[3] Stubbs was also dissatisfied with the copper plate as a medium for enamels – because of the size and weight consideration there was an upper limit (about 15 × 18 in)[4] for any miniature in copper. This did not appeal to Stubbs who was accustomed to painting some animals near life-size, leading him to look for an alternative support for enamels, one of his ideas being ceramic plaques. He approached Coade, the makers of artificial stone, who took no interest. However, the idea did come to the attention of Thomas Bentley, Josiah Wedgwood's partner, before 1775 when these three enquiring minds began to contemplate the manufacture of 'canvasses' for Stubbs. In Wedgwood's mind it appears to have been the start of a commercial venture.

> 'At present I think we should give Mr Stubbs every encouragement to proceed & establish the fashion. He wishes you know to do something for us by way setting off against the tablets. My picture and Mrs Wedgwoods in enamel will do something. Perhaps he may take your governess & you in by the same means. I should have no objection to a family piece, or rather two, perhaps, in oil, if he sho.d visit us this summer at Etruria.'[5]

Wedgwood hoped, no doubt, that these Queen's Ware plaques would be adopted by other artists and perhaps even make a profit by their sale.

Progress seems to have been slow on the tablets as a letter from Wedgwood to Bentley of 4 November 1777 explains: 'My compts to Mr Stubbs. He shall be gratified, but large tablets are not the work of a day'.[6]

On the 26 November, he writes:

'One or two of Mr Stubbs' tablets go into the kiln on Thursday next, but they are not large, abo.! 22 × 17. We are preparing larger but must proceed by gentle degrees'.[7]

Wedgwood fired three further tablets early in December, of which only one was successful. This he sent to the artist in London. It appears to have measured 22 × 17 in and is possibly the 'Lion attacking a Stag' which is signed and dated 1778.

The next year's production, however, was not so successful. In October 1778 the situation seems perilous.

'When you see Mr Stubs pray tell him how hard I have been labouring to furnish him with the means of adding immortality to his excellent pencil. I mean only to arrogate to myself the honor of being his *canvas maker* But alass this honor is at present denied to my endeavors, though you may assure him that I will succeed if I live a while longer undisturbed by the french as I only want an inclin'd plane that withstands our fire. My first attempt has failed, & I cannot well proceed in my experiments 'till we lay by work for xmas when our kilns will be at liberty for my trials.'[8]

The expense of the work was beginning to worry Wedgwood early in 1779. A letter from William Cox to William Brock in London expresses the potter's fears. 'Mr Wedgwood desires me to inform you that they are as yet great loses by selling them at the price fixed last year. Consequently they cannot think of selling them any lower'.[9] Seemingly Stubbs felt the price was too high and may have been finding some difficulties in paying.

The letter of 30 May 1779 seems to betoken a degree of success, especially as Wedgwood now sees the chance of a fashion for such plaques emerging. It must have been a costly triumph, for Wedgwood was most concerned over Stubbs' paying for not only the experimentation but the structural alterations necessitated in the kilns.

'Now I wish you to see Mr Stubbs & if the idea meets your approbation, to tell him that if it is convenient for him to pay in money for what he hitherto had, it will pay something towards the kilns, & alteration in kilns we have made & the other expenses we have been at in our essays, & the next £100 or £150 in tablets, perhaps more, shall be work & work, we will take the payment in paintings.'[10]

The next mention of Stubbs is in Wedgwood's letter to Bentley of 7 August 1780 when the artist is at Wedgwood's estate of Etruria. Thereafter, there is no mention of Stubbs' work on plaques in Wedgwood's letters save one. This is in some ways rather surprising as most of the extant plaques bear dates from 1780 to 1795, the year of the potter's death.

It may be that Wedgwood, after Bentley's death in November 1780, felt none of his other correspondents would be sufficiently interested in the project as he never mentioned it. That there is no correspondence between him and Stubbs is not surprising, for after 1780 Stubbs' connection with Wedgwood must have been direct and purely with the London establishment in Greek Street where he could collect plaques and presumably then have them fired in the enamelling kilns at the rear of the premises. Such a business relationship would preclude any need for direct correspondence.

As mentioned above, the 'Lion attacking a Stag' is the first known work by Stubbs on a Wedgwood plaque. The next two works are smaller ('Lion and dead Tiger', $17\frac{1}{4} \times 24$ in, 'Leopard', $7\frac{1}{2} \times 11$ in) and of rectangular format. These two works seem to imply some regression in Wedgwood's abilities to fire the plaques, although by the end of 1779 success seems to have been achieved.

'To Mr Bentley   Etruria 30th May 1779.
I wrote to you by post this morning, but wish to say a word or two concerning Mr Stubbs & his tablets.

We shall be able now to make them with certainty & success of the size of the 3 in this inv° & I hope to say as far as 30 inches – perhaps ultimately up to 36 inches by 24, but that is at present in the offing & I wo. not mention it to Mr Stubbs beyond 30 at present.

If Mr Stubbs succeeds he will be followed by others to which he does not seem to have the least objection but rather wishes for it; & if the oil painters too should use them they may become a considerable object.'[11]

Despite this hopeful note the next two known paintings in this medium, the portraits of Sarah and Josiah Wedgwood, are still smaller than the first work (20×16 in). In their limited palette both works strike one as experimental, especially in the flesh tones which have bubbled and cracked in a most unsightly manner in firing. I think it most likely that Stubbs produced them while he was at Etruria, when he could fire them under Wedgwood's expert supervision[12] and was able to obtain further plaques if the first ones proved faulty.[13]

The main purpose of Stubbs' visit to Etruria, according to Wedgwood in his letters to Bentley, was to paint the family portrait. Wedgwood originally wanted 'two family pieces' from Joseph Wright of Derby, but he seems to have been persuaded to employ Stubbs, especially as thereby he could recoup some of the expenses of the alterations to kilns and the experimentation needed to make the Queen's Ware plaques.

Despite Wedgwood's change of mind over the artist who was to execute the work he determined that Stubbs would paint the same subjects as Wright. No Renaissance patron laying down the iconography for his study could have been more precise in setting out in detail his exact desires.

'The two family pieces . . . . I mean to contain the children only & grouped perhaps in such manner as this. Sukey playing upon her harpsicord with Kitty singing to her which she often does, & Sally & Mary Ann upon the carpet in some employment suitable to their ages. This to be one picture. The pendant to be Jack standing at the table making fixable air with the glass apparatus &c; & his two brothers accompanying him. Tom jumping up and clapping his hands in joy & surprise at seeing the stream of bubbles rise up just as Jack has put a little chalk to the acid. Joss with the chemical dictionary before him in a thoughtful mood, which actions will be exactly descriptive of their respective characters.'[14]

Fine subjects for Joseph Wright with his mastery of interior light but hardly suitable for the more pastorally minded Stubbs.

The family portrait is one of the most important documented works by Stubbs, and one that caused some contention. It must have taken considerable pressure on the artist's part to persuade Wedgwood to abandon his original schemes in favour of a *plein-air* equestrian group portrait of the entire family. It is an ambitious work in which the artist has attempted to portray four principal equestrian figures and two smaller motifs: one of the younger children with a carriage; the other of Josiah and his wife Sarah, relaxing under a tree, in the company of the tripod table on which is proudly displayed a Wedgwood & Bentley Black Basalt vase, shape number one. The spire of Wolstanton church and the smoking bottle ovens fix the site of the portrait as the parkland surrounding Etruria Hall. The attempt to put so much narrative detail into the painting has made it a most disjointed work. Parts of it are beautiful – the skilful interrelationship of the horses' necks to the left of the picture has a natural subtlety which few of Stubbs' contemporaries could have matched. The disposition of the horses which were to 'sit' in the stable is obviously derived from the mares and foals paintings of two decades earlier, showing the positive delight which Stubbs has in demonstrating his knowledge of equine anatomy by displaying his horses in a frieze at all angles to the spectator. The portraits of Josiah, Sarah and Susannah are relaxed and graceful; Josiah II appears as an alert youth, swinging around in his saddle to look at the painter. Thomas's portrait in profile is most striking and has almost the effect of a classical medallion, a quality which the older Wedgwood no doubt appreciated. Unfortunately, John and the three young girls have the faces of wooden manikins. Indeed, it was this part of the painting which most disappointed Wedgwood.

'The children are most of them strong but not very delicate likenesses – some parts . . . . a little carictur'd'.[15]

However, Wedgwood to his credit, appreciated the problems which the artist like Stubbs faced, especially in such close contacts with his clients who demanded his time in many other pursuits.[16]

'Time and patience in large doses, are absolutely necessary in these cases & me thinks I would not be a portrait painter upon any conditions whatever, We are all heartily tired of the business & I think the painter has more reason than any of us to be so.'[17]

This close contact and the resulting intermittent working upon this painting must have caused Stubbs to lose his enthusiasm for it. The other tasks and commissions which interrupted it must have disturbed his sense of composition.

A more successful portrait which was executed at the same time as the family study is that of Richard Wedgwood, Sarah Wedgwood's father. This is also executed on panel and with its muted browns, greys and flesh tones is one of the most impressive and restrained of Stubbs' portrait studies, indeed it has a strong claim to being the finest portrait in Stubbs' oeuvre.

As Mr Taylor points out,[18] Stubbs was painting in a manner contrary to most of his contemporaries. Here, there is none of the impressionistic handling of Romney or even of Reynolds; instead there is a meticulously painted likeness which conveys its image, not by the use of broad brush strokes or impasto, but by the building up of small areas of paint in a way in which the brush strokes are barely perceptible. It is as if Stubbs was trying to follow the techniques of early Netherlandish Masters and emulating many effects of miniature enamellers. Wedgwood himself conceded that it was 'a very strong likeness' and he wanted a frame for it 'of a grave cast suitable to the age of the subject'.

When Wedgwood first mentions Stubbs' presence at Etruria on 7 August 1780 he indicated that some 'large jarrs have been made for Stubbs to paint on in enamels' and that they were pressing 'some clay tablets for modeling upon'. By the 13th Stubbs was ready to try his hand upon some of these vases but 'only for himself & friends' the results of which Wedgwood hoped would encourage the artist to produce some for commercial sale. Stubbs had also 'fixed upon his subject for modeling the *lion & horse* from his own engraving'.

This was selected despite other suggestions from Wedgwood who conceded that 'He does very well so far, & with little practice will probably be as much master of his modeling tools, as he is of his pencils'. By 21 August the modelling was finished and Wedgwood promises Bentley 'a copy very soon either in blue & white, or to save time in one colour' – no doubt in the hope of finding an eager metropolitan market.

The months of September and October were spent on the family portrait and other major commissions and it was not until the end of October that Stubbs resolved on the subject of the companion piece to the 'Frightened Horse' – the 'Fall of Phaeton'. Wedgwood objected to this as a companion piece to the 'Frightened Horse' – 'as that is a piece of natural history this is a piece of unnatural fiction.' He wished for something 'less hackney'd' although granted that 'it will be better to have that than nothing'. By 12 November the Phaeton 'is at some forwardness' as Stubbs obviously elated by his persuasive powers 'works hard at it every night almost "till bedtime".'

This information is in the last letter that Wedgwood ever wrote to Bentley, for the latter died on 26 November. Wedgwood in his letters to other friends never mentioned Stubbs and we do not know when the artist left Etruria, although his departure seemed imminent on the 12th; if he did any further work there, or if he ever returned.[19] There is no doubt that the collaboration continued until Wedgwood's death but no more direct account of it exists. There are no letters between the two, merely a note in Wedgwood's Commonplace Book and an account in the London ledger for some Queen's Ware which Stubbs bought. A letter in the Mayer Papers from Wedgwood to Peter Swift, the London accountant, of 6 May 1786, demonstrates that the plaques were still being provided and in some quantity.

> 'Enclosed is Mr Stubbs' account as it stands on our book, which is with the carriage charged as paid in London & no other, yet a bill may have been sent up with carriage charged at £2.1.9. This is wrong.'[20]

Such a high carriage charge, albeit wrongly levied, suggests that a large load was transported. In the same accumulation, there is a bill of 1796 showing that Stubbs had to wait until after the death of Wedgwood for his full payment for the work he did.

The note of 1788 gives a recipe for blue enamel to Stubbs which may demonstrate that the painter was still, at that late date, experimenting on his enamel palette.[21]

Wedgwood's Commonplace Book has an entry which could date from any time from 1786 to 1795 showing a payment as follows:[22]

To Mr. Stubbs Dr

Old men	170 guin
Family	184
Fathers port	20
	———
	374
	———

That these figures merely represent part payment is demonstrated by Stubbs'
bill in the Meyer papers

Family piece	236.17.6
Mrs. Wedgwood's father	26. 5.0
Mrs. Wedgwood	19.13.9
Labourers	189 0.0

£471.16.3

The 'old men' of the first bill is the 'Labourers' of the second which Stubbs painted for Wedgwood in 1781 again on a Queen's Ware plaque. It is fitting that
Wedgwood should have ordered a copy of the 'Labourers' for it was his seeing
this subject at the Royal Academy Exhibition of 1779 which was a factor in
persuading him to ask Stubbs to paint the family portrait in preference to
Wright.

The remainder of Stubbs' account is evidently a claim against Wedgwood for
faulty plaques as it appears that three out of a batch of five were damaged.

To 1781 belong also the 'Self-Portrait' (with the revealing sketch for it, demonstrating Stubbs' meticulous method of approach towards his work on
Queen's Ware), the 'Young Gentlemen Shooting' and the 'Stallions Fighting'.

1782 sees the production of 'Isabella Saltonstall in the character of Una', the
'Farmer's Wife and the Raven' and a self-portrait on horseback.

Only one painting on Queen's Ware is known from 1783. This, a portrait
of an elderly man in an attitude of study was previously unidentified. It is,
however, now fairly certain that it is of Erasmus Darwin and appears to have
been in the possession of the Darwin family in the 19th century. After the death
of Bentley, Darwin was Wedgwood's closest confidant so it is not surprising that
he should have been immortalised in such a way. There is then a prodigious gap
in the chronology of known works, the next known one being an equestrian
portrait of Warren Hastings, of 1791. To 1794 belongs the 'Haymakers' and
finally in 1795 appear the 'Reapers' and 'Hay Carting'.

It is interesting to speculate why there is such a large gap between the two
groups. There does not seem to be any technical problem in the production of
the plaques – the 'Farmer's Wife and Raven' and the self-portrait on horseback
are both of similar dimensions to the later works. However, there are differences
in the palette. The later works have more variety of colours and it seems likely
that Stubbs may have halted production in the mid-eighties to experiment
further upon enamel colours – the note of 1788 would give substance to this.
There was also the problem of the lack of control over the firing temperature

which could lead to the blistering of the enamel which was particularly notice-able in skin tones. If Stubbs wished to make his reputation with portraits painted in enamel colours then this was a very daunting problem. Indeed it may be the reason why all the major portraits in this medium belong to the early phase; possibly Stubbs found the difficulties insurmountable.

As it is most likely that the majority of the works were fired in the Wedgwood Greek Street premises, where they had an enamelling kiln, it is possible that the absence of Wedgwood's expert eye led to these and other faults appearing after the enamel firing.

The last of Stubbs' known works on Queen's Ware coincide with Wedgwood's death.[23] I think this is no coincidence, for in reality the venture was a failure for both.

As far as Stubbs went, the association had succeeded technically, to a degree; but the works he had shown in this medium failed to arouse critical approval when exhibited either at the Royal Academy or the Society of Artists[24] and most of them stayed unsold in his studio until his death. This must have been a bitter blow to Stubbs, especially after the poor placing of his five enamels at the 1782 Royal Academy exhibition which led directly to the artist not fulfilling his obligations to become a full academician. Their colours were apparently con-sidered too garish compared with the sombre hues of the work of the other ex-hibitors. Stubbs' meticulous approach was very much at variance with the bravura exhibited in the impasto of his contemporaries. This was a period in which the texture of the paint and the brush strokes were becoming increasingly important both to artist and client. In these circumstances a medium which by firing the paint into globules completely destroyed such effects could hardly seem attractive. Not only this but the high risk attendant upon the successful firing of the work must have dissuaded other artists. The chance that a painting which represented much work, effort and money to the artist could be destroyed through no fault of his own by the vagaries of a bottle oven must have militated strongly against any other artist adopting the idea. Not only that, but each plaque seems to have cost about ten pounds; far more than a panel or a canvas. So despite Stubbs' enthusiasm for others to follow where he had led, no other artist, not even those in Wedgwood's sphere such as Wright or Romney, could be induced to paint upon Wedgwood plaques. Wedgwood was on intimate terms with Reynolds, he had sat for him in 1781, had borrowed some of his designs, was a fellow member of the Royal Society and had persuaded him to write a letter of authentication for his copies of the Portland Vase, yet even here at the font of artistic honour there was no interest. Indeed, there seems to have been positive hostility. The late 18th century regarded Stubbs' work on Queen's

Ware as an aberration. Stubbs, who had hoped to establish his reputation as a portrait painter in this medium, became, instead, in the eighties and nineties, even more known as the 'horse painter' who should 'meddle not with Woman, nor with Man'. In the 1807 sale of the artist's effects the sums that the enamels on Wedgwood plaques realised were generally derisory.[25]

Wedgwood had championed Stubbs when he was at Etruria and he was a persuasive advocate. He had appreciated his talents to the extent of frequently acquiescing to the painter's demands (over the family portrait, then the two modelled reliefs.) He had introduced him to the local gentry, including Lord Gower, and had hoped that Stubbs would become again a fashionable artist.

Although Wedgwood insisted on Stubbs paying a realistic price for the plaques and for what, today, would be known as the 'research and development phase' I do not think it is valid to suppose that he hoped to make much profit out of the venture, even if he did attract other artists. The venture must have been a purely prestigious one in which Wedgwood doubtless hoped his pottery would be brought to the attention of the public through the success of Stubbs and other artists. It is pertinent as Mr Taylor points out, that no mention is made of Wedgwood when Stubbs exhibits his works. Wedgwood was a shrewd business-man and would, in all probability, want to avoid any public identification with Stubbs until the venture was successful. It is true that he wanted it to succeed but he had many other calls upon his time and energy, he was a realist and must have seen that there was little in the way of profit in it. Therefore what was Wedgwood's motivation? It was, I think, essentially scientific. He was a con-stant experimenter equipped with so much nervous energy that he could barely rest. It was the challenge which spurred Wedgwood to produce these plaques; no doubt the challenge was sweeter because of the others who had refused. The achievement was great. To make earthenware plaques of such dimensions and with a smooth surface and a minimum of warping was a considerable scientific accomplishment, and it was on this plane that Stubbs and Wedgwood must have established their rapport.

However, the potter's sons did not share this attitude. They must have seen the project as an unprofitable and, worse for them, unfashionable liaison with an artist who was considered *passé*.

John and Josiah II have a record of some benevolence towards the arts – but more to the next generation, of Coleridge and Blake, than the non-romantic Stubbs. Thus it would have been with some relief upon John's part when he paid Stubbs the £471.16.3 which his father owed him, thereby severing a con-nection which was unique in the history of art; a potter who wished to be an artist's 'canvas maker'.

[1] A memo appears in Wedgwood's first Common-place Book dated 1775 (E39.28408).
'tablets for Mr. Stubbs – The proportions he likes are 3 feet by 2 and 3 by 2′ 4″ – or in general 4 by 3 and 3 by 2.'

[2] The Ozias Humphry manuscript life of George Stubbs gives 1771 as the date for Stubbs' beginning to paint enamels. As the first known enamel is the 'Lion attacking the Horse' of 1769 which was exhibited at the Society of Art in 1770, this date must be incorrect.

[3] Humphry, op cit. Humphry further states that Stubbs discovered 19 of these enamels.

[4] Humphry gives this as the upper limit for copper plaques.

[5] J.W. to T.B. 30 May 1779. E26.18894.

[6] E25.18791.

[7] J.W. to T.B. E25.18797.

[8] J.W. to T.B. E26.18856.

[9] Mayer papers, Picton Library, Liverpool.

[10] E.26.18894.

[11] E26.18894.

[12] Presumably the 22 × 17 in plaque of 1777 was painted in London and enamel fired in the kiln behind the Wedgwood Greek Street premises.

[13] Even in 1796 Stubbs was complaining of faulty plaques; of five provided three were cracked – Mayer papers, op cit.

[14] J.W. to T.B. 30 May 1779 E26.18894.

[15] J.W. to T.B. 21 Oct 1780. L.H.P.

[16] Stubbs arrived at Etruria before 7 August 1780 and did not leave until after 12 November. He seems to have started work on the family portrait by 21 August by which time he had finished modelling in clay the 'Frightened Horse'. He seems then to have been at Etruria until 14 September when he went to Mr Swinnerton's where he remained until the 24th. In this period he finished a portrait of Mr and Mrs Swinnerton (40 × 50 in). On 8 October he was working on the family portrait and that of Wedgwood's father-in-law. On 28 October he was at Mr and Mrs Fitzwilliams and between then and 12 November was still engaged in their painting ($71 \times 47\frac{3}{4}$ in) plus the Wedgwood family portrait and his model of the 'Fall of Phaeton'. On 28 October Wedgwood did not consider the family portrait complete. Compared with the speed with which Stubbs completed two other large portraits, the family portrait seems to have occupied much time in irregular sessions punctuated by other commissions.

[17] J.W. to T.B. 21 October 1780. LH.P.

[18] Basil Taylor, Stubbs, Phaidon Press 1971, passim.

[19] Wedgwood family lore credits Stubbs with two further Etruria visits in the 1780s although there is no evidence to support this.

[20] Mayer papers, op cit.

[21] The recipe is for blue enamel, E11.9509.

[22] E.39.28410.

[23] And the removal to London establishment from Greek Street to York Street, St. James's, where initially there was no kiln.

[24] The Gentleman's Magazine expresses relief in 1791; 'We congratulate Stubbs on his pictures, and are happy to find the rage for enamel has so prudently subsided'. It continues hoping that the artist now 'mounted on his proper Pegasus . . . will never experience the disgrace which must be ever attendant on mounting his hobby horse of enamel portrait painting'.

[25] The Catalogue of all the remaining Valuable Collection of Original Paintings the Property and Performance of that ingenious and celebrated British Artist, George Stubbs, Esq., Dec, Peter Coxe 26, 27 May 1807' – Victoria and Albert Museum Library, annotated copy with prices.

Technical Aspects
of Stubbs' Enamel Painting

'Enamelling is proper only for pieces in miniature: it would be impossible to make any of a larger size without being subject to loss in some part of that quality of surface which is necessary, to hinder them from reflecting the light on several sides.

The accidents moreover to which they are exposed by the fire, increase in proportion to the surfaces, at least in a geometrical proportion, which alone is sufficient to discourage even the ablest artist.

Thus the project of executing large pieces in this kind of work must be always for this, and a hundred other reasons, a decisive proof of the ignorance of the person that undertakes it: nay it is certain, that all things equal the enamel loses its beauty by departing from a particular size; the fineness and minuteness of its execution would grow too tiresome to the spectator in large pieces, which indeed require another manner of painting more susceptible of freedom and ease.'

André Rouquet, *The present State of the Arts in England*, 1755

Much controversy has been raised about the exact techniques used by Stubbs and the body employed by Wedgwood for the ceramic plaques. The following comments are based on my own observations of almost all the existing works by Stubbs both on copper and ceramics, corroborated by the advice of Mr Stephen Rees-Jones of the Courtauld Institute, Mr John Hargrave, the picture restorer and Mr John Tindall, head of the technical department of Wedgwood, and by analyses conducted by the British Ceramic Research Association. It is hoped that this exhibition will provide scope for analysis of the works together which may lead to further findings.

It was entirely within the experimental nature of Stubbs' character that he should wish to paint enamels on copper, and to extend the range of colours which could be so used. The chemical experiments which he undertook must have been comprehensive and he seems, after three years, to have produced only small quantities of the pigments. It appears that with the copper enamels he followed the standard procedures of applying a white ground to the copper which was then fired. On this opaque white ground he would have painted in gouache-like pigments. The whole would have been fired again to fuse the enamels to the flux. The whole procedure required a high degree of temperature control to prevent the flux overwhelming the colours or the imperfect fusion of the pigments.

It has been suggested that he worked at one of the enamel factories at Bilston in order to gather information. This is not impossible although no information has emerged to substantiate this supposition. It may have been that the advice and assistance of Cosway was sufficient. The colours used by Stubbs in the copper enamels show little in the way of advance upon contemporary enamels, it is in the size and artistic sophistication that the contrast is seen. The effect of his works on copper is of a lustrous jewel-like surface in which the luminescence of the white ground shows through and the paint surface shows little or no sign of brush work.

Technically the copper enamels were a success; why therefore did he abandon them in favour of ceramic, for no copper enamels appear after 1775, the year of the start of the liaison with Wedgwood? Humphry hints that Stubbs wanted something larger on which to express his full painting abilities but I feel that is not all. The enamels on ceramic are more painterly, in the true sense of the word, than the ones on copper. Even though they are fired, the brush strokes and the texture of the paint remain. The whites are built up on the surface rather than being effected by allowing the ground to show through. In these works Stubbs gets the best of both the painting and enamel worlds, the texture of paint and the permanence of enamel colour. For conventional eighteenth-century paintings have become palimpsests, beset with restorations and colour changes; these are holograph. Even today their bright colours and contrasts are striking. In the eighteenth century they must have been profoundly disturbing when other masters were covering their works with a dark brown varnish.

It is possible that, as Humphry suggests[1], the copper experiments started out as a hobby, but the Wedgwood venture was far more serious – a 'hobby horse' in fact. Stubbs' intention was nothing less than the re-establishment of his reputation through this medium. Five out of seven of his works in the 1782 Royal Academy exhibition were enamels. Wedgwood, in a letter to Bentley of 25 September 1780 states that:

'Mr. S. repents much his having established this character for himself. I mean that of horse painter & wishes to be considered as an history and portrait painter. How far he will succeed in bringing about the change at his time of life I do not know. The exhibition may do wonders for him.'

Alas it did not. He seems to have effectively abandoned the portrait idea or maybe approached it very subtly! There were three portraits at the exhibition two of which had the sitters in landscapes with heads on a minute scale. The third was the Self-Portrait. The history aspect was equally weak, only the 'Una and the Lion' and the 'Farmers Wife and the Raven' could be said to even approach that category.

[1] The relevant section of Humphry's text appears on pp. 117-8

Wedgwood seems to have been working on parallel lines in the late 6os, the only patent he took out was for 'Encaustic' enamel colours for his neo-classical black basalt vases. He also seems, from his Experiment Books, to have been engaged in many enamel trials around 1773 possibly for the 'Frog' Service and the enamel of Etruria Hall (No. 4). As work like this must have found its way down to his London decorating establishments, then in Chelsea, it is not beyond the bounds of possibility that Stubbs may have seen and been impressed by such a piece by 'young Stringer'. It is intriguing to speculate how much cross fertilization there was between Wedgwood and Stubbs over enamel colours in the early '70s. A note in the London Experiment Book in the hand of Thomas Bentley (E22.19122) which can be dated on internal evidence to *c*.1777–8 shows that Stubbs may have been indulging in some 'industrial espionage' at second hand and passing on his information to Wedgwood.

'103) The best kind of Glass for mixing with colours. Melt equal parts of mineral alkali and white sand together for the space of two hours. Phlogisticate this mixture & you have a precious purple or rich red colour.

'Mr. Stubbs had this receipt given to him & he gave it to Mr. Mather as a valuable secret, the production being sold they say to enamel painters at Six Guineas an ounce'.

The note of 1788 shows that the traffic was not all one way and that Wedgwood was assisting Stubbs in his continued enamel experiments.

The composition used by Stubbs for his enamels must have of necessity changed with his transfer from copper to earthenware. The principle remained the same, that of a colouring agent suspended in a glassy medium which would be fixed on firing to the support to which it was applied, but the exact composition of the medium must have been different for the two supports. The reason for this difference lay in the higher firing temperatures used for copper as opposed to earthenware. The medium for copper consisted basically of lead, borax or potash and ground flint or other silicates, as did that for earthenware, but the proportions differed, and Wedgwood, as substantiated by his Experiment Books, frequently used fritted lead glass in preference to lead.

The Wedgwood plaques on which Stubbs worked all appear to be biscuit earthenware of a similar composition to his Queen's Ware, a light-weight body made up of clay and calcined flint. About 1774 Wedgwood was beginning to make a very white earthenware body which was even further whitened by the addition of china clay after the change in Champion's patent in 1775 which permitted the use of that material in non-translucent ceramic bodies.

The plaques would have been made by pressing cheese-hard clay into an oval matrix which would have been lifted off when the clay had dried and contracted.

The plaques would have then been fired in a biscuit oven on 'batts' of refractory clay, presumably upon Wedgwood's 'inclin'd plane' although the exact character of this device is not known.

The firing of the plaques must have required considerable work and the overcoming of many problems, as Wedgwood's letters show. One of the major obstacles must have been the tensions set up in such a large mass of clay during firing which would cause warping.

None of the tablets is an exact oval nor has a totally flat surface. The portrait of Josiah Wedgwood demonstrates this. At some time it was broken and it was impossible to obtain an exact register due to internal stresses when it was repaired with a result that some of the pieces stand proud from the rest of the picture surface. Such distortions would be less perceptible in an oval format than a rectangular one, which may account for the adoption of the former shape. It is unfortunate that no accounts survive of Wedgwood's work on these plaques. He was a most methodical potter, recording all his ceramic experiments and it is most likely that he kept a separate Experiment Book recording his work for Stubbs which has disappeared. All the plaques are slightly pitted on the back and show some signs of reactive impurities in small holes and black specks.

None of the plaques is glazed, a process which would have required a further firing. This would not have presented too much of a technical problem thus it may be assumed that Stubbs preferred the matt surface of the biscuit plaque to the glossy surface of a glazed one.

All the enamels on earthenware plaques are fired, they are most certainly not in oil colours.[1] Stubbs would have initially painted in enamels which would have appeared similar to gouache and the resulting painting left to dry. At this stage if what Humphry says is correct, Stubbs sought pigments such that the colours of the unfired work would have been approximately the same as those when it was fired. As ceramic enamel colours tend to lighten with an increase in heat, precise temperature control would have been necessary.

It is noticeable that the palette becomes more varied through the years and that in all the works evidence of brush strokes can be seen. To date all the Barlaston enamels have been examined under the microscope showing positive evidence of firing. This evidence is most noticeable to the naked eye in the imperfectly fused colours which are in their original state very pitted.

[1] Two of three enamels at Barlaston have been examined. No. 9, under the microscope at the Courtauld laboratories, showed fused particles of enamel on the surface. No. 12 was thoroughly tested by the British Ceramic Research Association, who concluded that the body of the plaque was a low-fired earthenware containing flint, and the paint surface was enamel containing alumina and silica with traces of calcium and potash, which had been fired. Although not scientifically analysed, the others appear to have similar characteristics.

Enamels

The word 'enamel' is used to denote both a material and various forms of pictorial art which are made from it.

The material is essentially a kind of glass formed from silicates with minium and potash or borax, tinted by a range of metallic oxides according to the colour required, and attached through heating in a kiln to metal or ceramic supports, according to the nature of the particular technique. Its use has been long and widespread and seems to have appeared first in ancient Assyrian and Egyptian art, where it was applied on a substantial scale to bricks and pottery, and, in small amounts, in the making of jewellery.

The chief forms of enamelling technique are as follows:

Champlevé enamels are achieved by cutting troughs in a metal plate so that the raised parts between form the outline of the design, the enamel being formed in the depressions between.

Cloisonné enamels use thin metal strips soldered to a sheet of metal to define the design, the enamel being formed within the areas thus created.

Bassetaille The enamel is here applied as a transparent layer over a metal surface which has previously been engraved and worked in relief.

In all these techniques the pulverised enamel 'pigments' are placed on the surface of the support and attached to it by firing in the kiln.

Painted enamels result, as their name implies, in effects similar to those to be obtained by the use of oil colours applied thinly to a smooth support. In the case of this technique the plate first receives a layer of white enamel upon which the design is painted in grisaille or colours. A second firing is then used to fuse the design to this ground, the colours sometimes having a small admixture of the vitreous material mentioned above, sometimes, as normally in miniature portraits in this medium, being simply the metallic oxides.

Stubbs' works exhibited here are *painted enamels*. In those on a copper plate the pigments applied to the white ground would have had only a small amount of the vitreous material in the colours; in those made on ceramic tablets the amount of the vitreous material would have had to be increased to suit the character of the ceramic support.

Basil Taylor

1 *Preliminary measured drawing for the 'Anatomy of the Horse'*

Ink on paper, $14\frac{1}{4} \times 19\frac{3}{4}$ in
Inscr: 'Proportions taken from the skeleton of an old mare about 13 hands
high./NB the centre portion in the junctions of the vertebrae of the neck (from
the joining of the 2 with the 3 to the joining of the 4th with the first of ye back
has directly (?) the anterior part of the bodies and position (?) (?) of the
descending oblique passages in a line drawn from the interior parts of these two
places.'
Prov: Bequeathed by Stubbs to Mary Spencer, sold to Colnaghi on her death,
1817; bought by Sir Edwin Landseer who bequeathed them to Charles
Landseer who bequeathed them to the Royal Academy of Arts.
Not previously exhibited.
Lit: Parker, p. 24.
Royal Academy of Arts

This drawing demonstrates the meticulous approach which Stubbs applied to
his work. The exact measurements and the comments on various proportions
suggest that he was trying to establish some kind of mathematical formula for
the anatomy of the animal, something which he attempts again much later in
the *Comparative Anatomy*. Such a scientific approach which searches for knowledge *per se* rather than purely as an aid to more accurate reproduction is
paralleled in his enamel experiments, putting Stubbs next to Leonardo da Vinci
as the greatest painter-scientist in history. Stubbs' belief in perspective, which he
had once taught, strengthens his link with the scientific approach of the
Quattrocento.

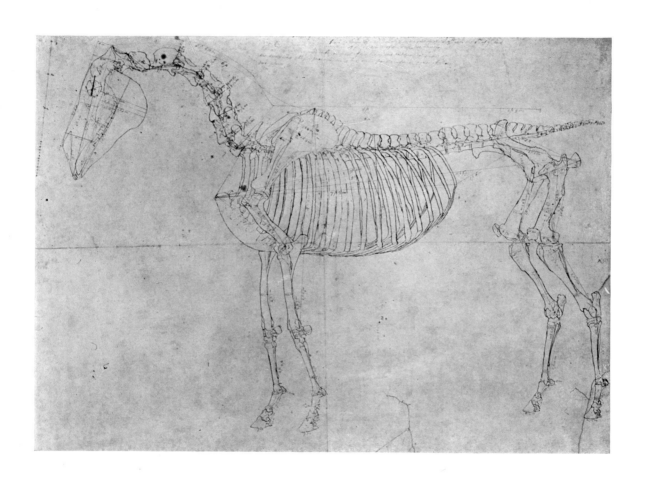

2 *Two preliminary drawings for the 'Anatomy of the Horse'*

Chalk on paper, each $14\frac{1}{2} \times 7\frac{1}{2}$ in
Prov: Bequeathed by Stubbs to Mary Spencer, sold to Colnaghi on her death,
1817; bought by Sir Edwin Landseer who bequeathed them to Charles
Landseer who bequeathed them to the Royal Academy of Arts.
Exh: Whitechapel, 1957 (57–74); Virginia Museum, 1960.
Lit: Parker, p. 24.
Royal Academy of Arts

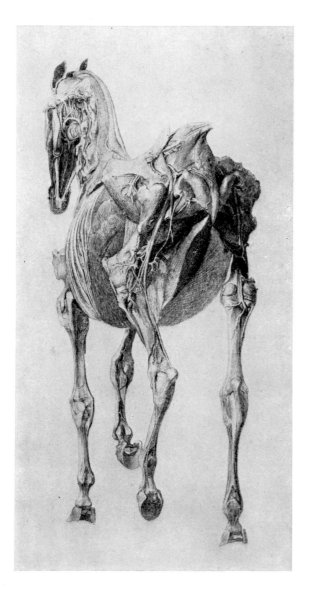
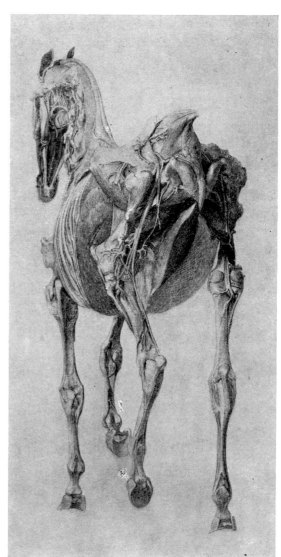

3 *Mares and Foals in a Landscape*

Oil on canvas, $40 \times 63\frac{3}{4}$ in
Prov: Family of the Earl of Middleton who sold it to the Tate Gallery 1959.
Exh: Liverpool, 1951 (36); Whitechapel, 1957 (32); *Stubbs in the 1760's,*
Agnews, 1970 (7).
Lit: Taylor (4); Parker.
Tate Gallery

'Mares and Foals in a Landscape' belongs to a series of paintings of this subject mostly executed in the period 1760–9. The frieze-like disposition of the horses is typical and is echoed in the Wedgwood Family portrait (12) which has far closer affinities with this series of paintings than with Stubbs' other equestrian conversation pieces.

Attributed to EDWARD STRINGER (fl. 1770–1783)

4 *Etruria Hall*

Enamel on Wedgwood biscuit earthenware, $7\frac{1}{2} \times 14\frac{1}{2}$in
Prov: Found on Etruria Works, 1905.
Lit: Williamson; Mayer; Heaton Hall Bicentenary.
Trustees of the Wedgwood Museum, Barlaston

This painting of Etruria Hall appears to be the original work from which the view of the house on the Wedgwood 'Frog' service, made for Catherine the Great in 1773–4, was derived.

Edward Stringer appears to have been a distant relation of Wedgwood, whose mother was a Stringer. He was one of the family of Knutsford Stringers which included Samuel, James the architect and Daniel.

There is a mention of a Stringer in a letter from Wedgwood to Bentley of 19 November 1767 where he says that he had met 'Mr. Stringer the Painter' in Knutsford whom he had invited to Burslem to paint a 'Groupe of figures' of 'Mr. & Mrs. Willet & their four Girls & perhaps our Children to fill up with'. This Mr. Stringer is 'good natur'd modest & ingenious' and appears also to be willing to help out in the design of ornamental ware. However this paragon is more likely to have been Samuel Stringer who exhibited at the Liverpool Society of Artists in 1774 (Mayer p. 28) and was dead by 1784 according to the Liverpool Exhibition catalogue of that year, or perhaps Daniel, who was listed as a portrait painter in the latter catalogue.

'Young Stringer' is first mentioned by Wedgwood in a letter to Bentley of 29 April 1770:—

'I am told young Stringer of Knutsford is coming to Town to see the exhibition & draw at the Academy etc.'

'You know what I mean by painting Vases so if he shod call you will know how to act with him.'

Here Stringer appears as the prototype for Stubbs and his 'large jarrs' for painting on. Stringer spent much of the summer and autumn of 1773 at Etruria whence he travelled drawing views for the 'Frog' service with Wedgwood speculating as to whether he should be hired 'for a few months to paint & instruct our hands in London'.

In a letter of 4 November Wedgwood states that he has some views by Stringer for the service 'two from Trentham . . . . one from Mr. Mill's & one from Etruria'. The evidence of the letters combined with the similarity of this painting to the view of Etruria Hall in the service substantiates an attribution to young Stringer. Stylistically this work is in the same manner as several signed

T? E? F? S? Stringer, portraits of dogs, horses, etc. which exist in this hand (Heaton Bicentenary p. 75).

There is no evidence in the letters as to the exact identity of 'young Stringer'. However, other letters in the Wedgwood archives from one Edward Stringer of Lichfield, a painter, show a long standing relationship. A letter from him to Wedgwood of 1781 refers to 'past favours' and a bill of November 1783 is for £20 which must be for quite substantial work, far more than the 'Blank Windows' which he was executing for Etruria that August.

It seems therefore that 'young Stringer' may have under Wedgwood's aegis experimented in enamel colours on earthenware plaques. The colours of this painting are very successful, comparable to the 19 Stubbs was producing concurrently, demonstrating that Wedgwood's knowledge of the colour changes inherent in enamel firing was considerable. It is likely that Wedgwood felt he could not 'establish the fashion' with Stringer whom he considered 'a sad, untutor'd raw young fellow' and by implication of very limited talent. This work does show, however, that Wedgwood had a great interest in such enamels before the start of the liaison with Stubbs about 1775. The idea was already in his mind and no doubt he considered Stubbs to be more promising than Stringer.

JOSIAH WEDGWOOD, FRS (1730–1795)

4a *Two Trays of Experiments*

Although no actual experiments or records of experiments survive for the work Wedgwood undertook for Stubbs, it is likely that the two suites of experiments may be relevant. The first is a series employing clay 'from the estate of the Duke of Athol'.

Parallel to the production of plaques to paint upon, Wedgwood was also trying to produce pallettes for Stubbs in Queen's Ware. These were apparently too heavy and Wedgwood asks Bentley (JW to TB 18 Oct 1777) to obtain some more of 'a light earth' which they had in the past obtained from the Duke. It is not until 4 November 1780 that 'little pallets' are ready. These and larger ones seem to have been prepared 'under Mr. Stubbs directions'.

The large size of the plaques made for Stubbs to paint upon would have encouraged Wedgwood to make them of a light material. Therefore, the experiments upon the Duke of Atholl's clay may have been a factor in their production.

Wedgwood, like all potters of the period, was much concerned with the procuring of enamels which would give constant colour values upon firing. There seems to have been considerable interchange of information between him and Stubbs on this mutually interesting subject. The notes of 1777–8 and of 1788 are probably only two of many.

Many of the enamel colours used by Stubbs have a matt surface, a quality which Wedgwood needed and obtained for his red-figure 'Etruscan' vases. The years of 1781–3 saw Wedgwood experimenting on colours and 'Unglossy enamel'. Another experiment book (E.26.19124A) has a section dated 31 August 1782 entitled 'Experiments for ascertaining a set of good Enamel Colours'. Here references are made to various London Experiment Books, which no longer exist. As most of the enamel decorating was executed in the metropolis it is only to be expected that the experiments would have been done there. How much Stubbs helped in these experiments and how much Wedgwood taught him remains unknown. Suffice it to say that the enamels in which the Queen's Ware plaques are painted by Stubbs differ from those he used upon copper. We do not know from where he obtained his copper enamel recipes but on circumstantial evidence it may be suggested that Stubbs must have spent some time studying enamel techniques in the Wedgwood Greek Street premises around the end of the 1770s and the early 1780s, at which period Wedgwood himself was conducting similar experiments.

N.º

406 ⁷⁄₆ – 4 Gr.ᵗ · · · This seems to separate
part is run thin like water and is a good color, or
rather no color at all; the other thicker part is
greenish.

407 ⁷⁄₆ – 4 Gr.ᵗ · · · Much the same but
less of the watery part.

408 ⁷⁄₆ – 4 Gr.ᵗ · · · Much the same but
less still of the exuded watery part.

409 ⁷⁄₆ – 4 Gr.ᵗ Rather better.
69

410 ⁷⁄₆ 4 – 3½ Gr.ᵗ Worse color but
Fired   not separated like the above N.ᵒˢ
is more of an uniform Glass but not clear; is
what we call Scummy on the surface

411 ⁷⁄₆ – 4 Gr.ᵗ

A good W.ᵐ Glass!

The best of all these trials — Uniform.
Transpar.ᵗ and nearly colorless.

412 ⁷⁄₆ – 4
736 4

Nearly the same.

N.B. 412 and the preceding are not
quite beginning at the trials together
going from left to right

Ozias Humphry r.a. (1743–1810)

5 *George Stubbs*

Watercolour, 20 × 15¾ in
Prov: G. T. Stubbs; Mr Stamford; bought by the National Portrait Gallery,
1905.
Lit: Taylor (1); Parker.
Trustees of the National Portrait Gallery

Once thought to be a self-portrait of Stubbs, it shows the artist standing proudly beside his largest known enamel work on copper 'Fall of Phaeton' which is signed and dated 1775. It would be likely, therefore, that this portrait was executed between that year and 1778, the year of the first successful ceramic plaque.

A letter of 1905 in the National Portrait Gallery records that Mr Stamford of East Hill, Wandsworth, has two 'very large enamels by Stubbs, a Lion and Tiger fighting and a Horse and Lion fighting size about 24 × 18 oval'.

6 *Mother and Child, 1772*

Enamel on copper, 12 × 12 in, circular
Inscr: 'Geo. Stubbs pinxit 1772.'
Prov: H. E. Backer, Esq, sold to Basil Taylor, sold to Arthur Ackerman & Son
Ltd, sold to Sabin Galleries Ltd, who presented it to the Tate Gallery through
the Friends of the Tate Gallery, 1965.
Lit: Taylor (1).
Tate Gallery

Sold at the 1807 sale (90), second day, 8 guineas.

It is likely that the subject of the painting is Stubbs' mistress, Mary Spencer, and
their son George Townley Stubbs. Although the latter was born in 1756 it is not
unlikely that Stubbs would have executed many sketches of him when a child.

In Humphry's biography Mary Spencer is described as 'Mr Stubbs' female
relation and friend' with a note added stating she was his aunt. Upcott,
Humphry's natural son, who re-transcribed the memoir, makes her his niece.
She and Stubbs were constant companions for forty years and her status was
given as spinster when Stubbs' will was proved.

7 *Hope Nursing Love, 1774*

Enamel on copper, 12 in, circular
Inscr: 'Geo. Stubbs pinxit 1774'
Prov: Gift of H. I. Backer, Esq, to the Victoria & Albert Museum.
Lit: Taylor (1).
Trustees of the Victoria and Albert Museum

This is the work which was number 81 on the second day of the 1807 sale when it fetched 5 guineas.

There are close similarities with the 'Mother and Child' (6) and it is likely that the sitters are again Mary Spencer and George Townley Stubbs.

8 *Lion and Lioness, 1770*

Enamel on copper, $9\frac{1}{2} \times 11$ in, octagonal
Inscr: 'Geo Stubbs pinxit 1770'
Prov: Not known.
Exh: Society of Artists, 1771 (153?) 'A Lion and Lioness'.
Lit: Taylor (1, 4).
Private collection

This painting was lot 79 on the second day of the 1807 sale when it fetched £26.5.0.

9 *Josiah Wedgwood, 1780*

Enamel on Wedgwood biscuit earthenware, 20 × 16in, oval
Inscr: 'Geo. Stubbs pinxit 1780'
Prov: Painted for Josiah Wedgwood who bequeathed it to his son Josiah II;
sold ?1828–9; bought by Hensleigh Wedgwood after 1844; Frances Julia
Wedgwood; Elizabeth Hope Wedgwood; the Wedgwood Museum.
Exh: Wedgwood bicentenary exhibition, Hanley, 1930; Whitechapel, 1957.
Lit: Farrer; Finer & Savage; McKendrick; Parker; Taylor (1, 4).
Trustees of the Wedgwood Museum, Barlaston

Much debate has been occasioned by the inclusion of two portraits of Josiah
and Sarah Wedgwood in the 1807 sale of the artist's effects (lot 63, first day,
£2.5.0) as to whether there were two versions of these. Mr Taylor thinks that
this is unlikely. However, the evidence can be interpreted differently. The letter
of 30 May 1779 demonstrates that Wedgwood wanted portraits by Stubbs of
himself and Mrs Wedgwood.

'At present I think we should give Mr Stubbs every encouragement to
proceed & establish the fashion. He wishes you know to do something for us
by way setting off against the tablets. My picture & Mrs Wedgwoods in
enamel will do something'.

In this context it is likely that any portrait of Wedgwood could have been so
offset, although the one of Sarah was paid for in 1796 (£19.13.9). At that time
therefore, it is most likely that a pair of portraits were in the possession of the
family. The pair in the Wedgwood Museum appear to have come into the
Wedgwood family in the mid 19th century (that Francis Wedgwood in 1844 did
not know of their existence is indicated in a letter to Joseph Mayer) and the
most likely date for the disposal of the original pair is 1828/9 at the time of the
sale of the Wedgwood London showrooms and stock when the firm was in
extreme economic difficulties.

Thus, although it is not certain that the pair bought by Hensleigh Wedgwood
was the original pair belonging to Josiah I, it certainly seems that when a pair
was sold in 1807 the original pair was still in the possession of Josiah II.

It was not unusual for Stubbs to produce more than one version of a subject as
with the 'Labourers' and several others of his enamel compositions. The detailed
drawings which he produced for similar works would have made this fairly easy.
It is possible that the pair in the 1807 sale may have been intended for Bentley
as a memento of the leading part he played in introducing Stubbs to Wedgwood.
As Bentley died in 1780 the *raison d'etre* for such a pair would have been lost.

10 *Sarah Wedgwood, 1780*

Enamel on Wedgwood biscuit earthenware, 20 × 16in, oval
Inscr: 'Geo. Stubbs pinxit 1780'
Prov: Painted for Josiah Wedgwood who bequeathed it to his son Josiah II;
sold ?1828–9; bought by Hensleigh Wedgwood after 1844; Frances Julia
Wedgwood; Elizabeth Hope Wedgwood; the Wedgwood Museum.
Exh: Wedgwood bicentenary exhibition, Hanley, 1930; Whitechapel, 1957.
Lit: Farrer; Finer & Savage; McKendrick; Parker; Taylor (1, 4).
Trustees of the Wedgwood Museum, Barlaston

11 *Labourers, 1781*

Enamel on Wedgwood biscuit earthenware, $27\frac{1}{2} \times 36$ in, oval
Inscr: 'Geo. Stubbs pinxit 1781'
Prov: Painted for Josiah Wedgwood.
Lit: Mayer; Taylor (1, 3, 4)
Private Collection

It was the original version of this work in oil which Wedgwood saw at the Royal Academy in 1779 that inspired him to commission Stubbs to execute the Family Portrait.

The position over the enamel version of the 'Labourers' is confusing. Humphry and Mayer state that the original version in this medium was 28×36 in oval and a version painted for Erasmus Darwin was 30×42 in oval. However, in 1846 the latter's son, Dr Robert Waring Darwin, had in his possession a version, the dimensions of which corresponded to the original. The letter to Mayer, giving these facts is in the hand of Josiah Wedgwood III who does not seem to be aware of any other version.

This painting was formerly at Leith Hill Place, the home of Josiah III; thus it could have been one of the paintings he inherited from his father on the latter's death in 1843, although it is strange that he makes no mention of the fact in the letter to Mayer. It is more likely that his wife Caroline (*née* Darwin) may have inherited it. The tone of his letter is most helpful, he gives measurements for the 'Labourers' and informs Mayer that the Wedgwood family portrait is in the possession of his brother Francis.

As with the other Wedgwood paintings the 'Labourers' was paid for in instalments; 170 guineas, followed by £189 in 1796.

Other versions, oil on panel and the original, oil on canvas dated 1779, exist.

12 *Erasmus Darwin, 1783*

Enamel on Wedgwood biscuit earthenware, $26 \times 20\frac{1}{2}$ in, oval
Inscr: 'Geo. Stubbs pinxit 1783'
Prov: Darwin family.
Exh: Alton Towers, 1865, '93 Dr Darwin After Wright of Derby in the
possession of Elizabeth Darwin.'; Wedgwood Memorial Institute, 1869,
'143 Dr Darwin, Wright of Derby in the possession of Reginald Darwin.'
Trustees of the Wedgwood Museum, Barlaston

This previously unrecorded enamel by Stubbs was only positively identified as
one of his works in 1972 when the frame in which the painting was kept was re-
moved and the signature exposed. The sitter was at first unidentified, although
it was granted that it had more than a passing resemblance to the Wright
portrait of Erasmus Darwin in the National Portrait Gallery. This latter
portrait entered the Gallery Collection in 1859 so it cannot be the work mentioned in either the 1865 or the 1869 catalogue. From letters in the National
Portrait Gallery it also appears that no other portrait of Erasmus Darwin by
Wright was then in the possession of the Darwin Family. Susan Elizabeth
Darwin died in 1866 and no Reginald Darwin appears to exist (this may be a
misprint for [Charles] Robert Darwin).

Neither catalogue gives measurements or format of the work but it seems that
this is the Stubbs painting which had become wrongly identified as by Wright.
This is no uncommon fault in these two catalogues. The Stubbs family portrait
is correctly catalogued in the first work, but by 1869 it has become 'by Wright of
Derby' although still in the possession of Francis Wedgwood! If this can happen
with a painting prominently signed how much easier would it have been with a
work which bore a close resemblance to one by the Derby master. Erasmus
Darwin had a known interest in the enamel works of Stubbs (see No. 11) which
strengthens this identification.

13 *Richard Wedgwood, 1780*

Oil on panel, 28 × 23 in
Inscr: 'Geo. Stubbs pinx 1780'
Prov: Painted for Josiah Wedgwood; by descent to Dr Ralph Vaughan-
Williams who bequeathed it to the Wedgwood Museum, 1944.
Exh: Liverpool, 1951; Whitechapel, 1957.
Lit: Farrer; Finer & Savage; McKendrick; Taylor (1, 4); Parker.
Trustees of the Wedgwood Museum, Barlaston

Richard Wedgwood (1701–1782), Josiah Wedgwood's father-in-law was a
prosperous merchant of Spen Green, Cheshire.

   Stubbs was paid twenty guineas for this work followed by £26.5.0 paid by
John Wedgwood in 1796.

14 *The Wedgwood Family, 1780*

Oil on panel, $47\frac{1}{2} \times 59\frac{1}{2}$ in
Inscr: 'Geo. Stubbs pinxit 1780'
Prov: Painted for Josiah Wedgwood; by descent through the family to
Phoebe Wedgwood who bequeathed it to the Wedgwood Museum, 1968
Exh: Alton Towers, 1865; Wedgwood Memorial Institution, 1869; Wedgwood
bicentenary exhibition, Hanley, 1930; Liverpool, 1951.
Lit: Farrer; Finer & Savage; McKendrick; Parker; Taylor (1, 4).
Trustees of the Wedgwood Museum, Barlaston

The portrait shows the entire family in the grounds of Etruria Hall. They are
from right to left:

    Josiah I (1730–1795)
    Sarah (1734–1815)
    John (1766–1844)
    Josiah II (1769–1843)
    Susannah (1765–1817)
    Catherine (1774–1823)
    Thomas (1771–1805)
    Sarah (1776–1850)
    Mary Ann (1778–1786)

Both Stubbs and Wedgwood showed their concern with minutiae in the debate
they had concerning a suitable frame. Bentley was entrusted 'to look in Leicester
Square' for a frame leaving it to his and Mrs Bentley's taste. Wedgwood prepared a new model in November of which Stubbs so approved that 'he will adapt it
for his enamel picture of the largest size' Bentley was to take the new model to
the frame maker Mr Viel, Viels or Fiel.

Wedgwood expressed continual dissatisfaction with the painting 'my wife I
think very deficient – Mary Ann more so, & Susan is not hit off well at all'.
Perhaps this is why he paid Stubbs only 184 guineas in his lifetime with a
further £236.17.6 being paid by John after the potter's death.

15 *Lion Devouring a Horse, 1769*

Enamel on copper, $9\frac{1}{2} \times 11$ in, octagonal

Inscr: 'Geo Stubbs pinxit 1769'; on reverse, 'Nº J [? for 1]'

Prov: Penniston Lamb, 1st Viscount Melbourne; his daughter, firstly Lady Cowper, secondly Lady Palmerston; her son Lord Mount Temple; bought 1920 by Sir George Buckstone Browne and presented with Down House to the British Association for the Advancement of Science, by whom handed over to the Royal College of Surgeons 1952; sold 1968 to Speelman; sold to a private British collector, by whose executors sold to the Tate Gallery through the Maas Gallery.

Exh: Society of Artists, 16 April 1770, 'A lion devouring a horse, painted in enamel', (135); Whitechapel, 1957 (51).

Lit: Gilbey; Mayer; Taylor (1, 2, 4).

Tate Gallery

This appears to be Stubbs' first work in enamel and predates Humphry's statement that the collaboration between Stubbs and Cosway began in the early years of the 70s. Horace Walpole seeing it at the Society of Artists considered it 'very pretty'. According to Humphry, 'An octagon within a circle of 12 inches of a Lyon devouring a Horse was sold to Lord Melbourne for 100 guineas being the first picture in Enamel that our author sold.'

16 *Fall of Phaeton, 1775*

Enamel colours on copper, $14\frac{3}{4} \times 18$ in, oval
Inscr: 'Geo Stubbs pinxit 1775'
Prov: unknown
Exh: British Institution, 1806 (84).
Lit: Taylor (1, 4).

This painting, lot 89 on the second day, fetched the highest price of any work in the 1807 sale (310 guineas) where it is listed as 'Phaeton, a beautiful enamel on copper, and very highly finished conceived with Poetic Fire, and the action of the etherial coursers in their rapid progress, highly characteristic of the celebrated story'.

The engraving which Stubbs used as the source for his clay 'Fall of Phaeton' appears to have been based on this enamel.

17 *Fall of Phaethon*

Mezzotint engraving, $17\frac{1}{2} \times 21\frac{3}{4}$ in
Lit: Taylor (3)
Trustees of the British Museum

This subject was chosen by Stubbs to be modelled as the companion to the 'Frightened Horse'. Evidently the artist had not brought a copy of this mezzotint with him as Bentley is requested to obtain a copy in London.

(Stubbs) 'wishes to employ some of his evenings in modeling a companion to his frighten'd horse, & has fixed upon one of his Phaetons for that purpose, but cannot proceed till he has the print of this subject which he says may be had at some of the print shops, but he does not know which. There are two prints of Phaetons, in that which he would have the two *nearest* horses are fighting, in that which he would not have the middlemost, or farthest are fighting. He desires Mr Brock will find him this print & send it down by the first coach that he may have time to complete the model whilst he stays here'.

18 *Fall of Phaeton*

Solid blue Jasper, white relief, $10\frac{1}{2} \times 19\frac{3}{8}$ in
Inscr: (impressed mark) Wedgwood c. 1785.
Prov: Lord Tweedmouth; Lady Lever Art Gallery.
Exh: R.A. Winter Exh. 1934; Victoria and Albert Museum, Bicentenary 1959
(100).
Lit: Parker.
Trustees of the Lady Lever Art Gallery, Port Sunlight

By 28 October Stubbs had decided, to Wedgwood's displeasure, on this subject
as the companion to the 'Frightened Horse'. He required a copy of his own
etching (No. 17) before commencing, and Mr Brock of Wedgwood's London
establishment is requested to obtain it.

19 *Plaque with Nineteen Horse Studies*

Solid Green Jasper, white reliefs, 15 × 11 in, oval
Inscr: (impressed mark) 'WEDGWOOD' and 'O' (for Bert Bentley)
Prov: Etruria Factory.
Lit: Jean Gorley, *Old Wedgwood*, No. 10, Boston, 1943; Gunnis,
English Sculpture, London, 1951.
Trustees of the Wedgwood Museum, Barlaston

A ledger entry for 1788/9 exists giving 'Mr Burch's Bill' including '18 horses at 16s each'.

Edward Burch, R.A. (1730–1814) appears, originally, to have been a waterman. 'His first attempt in painting was exercised in the imitation of a gold band round his hat and the superior style of the interior of his wherry.' (*New Monthly Magazine*, 1816, p. 417).

He is chiefly known as a gem engraver and wax modeller. His early career seems to have been successful. Entering the Royal Academy School in 1769, he became an associate in 1770 and a full member a year later. In 1788 he was appointed gem engraver to the King and the Duke of York. In 1794 he became the librarian to the Academy and two years later was in such financial difficulties that the Academy made him a gift of £100.

His work for Wedgwood included reliefs of King George III and Queen Charlotte, eighteen dogs, a large dog, the signs of the zodiac, and Wedgwood's Seal. He also modelled an Intaglio for Tassie of the 'Frightened Horse' also after Stubbs.

Several of the horses depicted in these reliefs are identifiable as being after Stubbs, from known works. However, as these reliefs pre-date any of the engravings except in the case of the 'Frightened Horse' (centre, second from top) which is reversed from the painting, like the engraving. It appears that either Wedgwood or Burch must have obtained drawings by Stubbs in order to model these reliefs. The centre relief of a horse jumping a gate is, for example, very similar to one in an identical pose in the 'Charlton Hunt' of the early 1760s which was never engraved.

20 *Horse Frightened by a Lion*

Oil on canvas, $27\frac{3}{4} \times 40\frac{7}{8}$ in
Not inscribed
Prov: Not known
Lit: Taylor (2, 4); Parker.
Private collection

This appears to be the version of this subject from which Stubbs took his engraving (No. 21). This, in turn was used by the artist as the basis for his clay bas-relief of the 'Frightened Horse' which he modelled at Etruria.

21 *Frightened Horse*

Etching, $13\frac{1}{2} \times 18\frac{1}{4}$ in
Lit: Taylor (3)
Trustees of the British Museum

It is possible that Stubbs brought a copy of this engraving with him to Etruria
in 1780 for use in the modelling of the ceramic 'Frightened Horse'.

22 *Six Buttons with Horse Studies*

White Jasper blue dip, with white reliefs *c.* 1790, $1\frac{1}{2}$ in, diameter
Not inscribed.
Prov: Calland Collection
Exh: Wedgwood at Woburn, 1973 (W7)
Lit: Jean Gorley, *Old Wedgwood*, No. 10, Boston, 1943; Gunnis, *English Sculpture*,
London, 1951.
Trustees of the Wedgwood Museum, Barlaston

23 *The Frightened Horse*

a Plaster mould for the prototype
b Modern version from *a*, black basalt
c Production version, black basalt
Prov: Etruria Factory.
Lit: McKendrick; Parker.
Trustees of the Wedgwood Museum, Barlaston

On 1 August 1780 clay tablets had been prepared for Stubbs to model on and by
the 13th the artist had chosen his subject

‘he is now laying in the horse whilst I am writing a few letters this good
Sunday morning’.

By 21st he had finished it and Wedgwood was promising Bentley a copy ‘very
soon either in blue & white, or to save time in one colour’.

The existence of the mould *a* demonstrates that an original version was
prepared which contained far more background detail than the one which was
finally produced. It is likely that Wedgwood considered this prototype too
complex for production. A blue and white Jasper version marked ‘WEDG-
WOOD & BENTLEY’ was in the Oster Collection. This was identical to the
Basalt version shown here. As Bentley died in November of 1780, the Oster
piece is evidence that the first ‘Frightened Horses’ must have been as *c* and that
the prototype must have been abandoned.

24 *Young Gentleman Shooting, 1781*

Enamel on Wedgwood biscuit earthenware, $18 \times 24\frac{1}{2}$ in, oval
Inscr: 'Geo Stubbs pinxit 1781'
Prov: Collection of Sir Walter Gilbey, Bart; his executors' sale, Christie's,
11 June, 1915 (405).
Exh: Royal Academy, 1782 (79), Agnews, 1959.
Lit: Taylor (1, 4).
Private Collection

Basil Taylor has suggested that the subject is Mr Huth, as mentioned by
Humphry.

25 *Miss Isabella Saltonstall*
as Una in Spenser's Faerie Queene, 1782

Enamel on Wedgwood biscuit earthenware $18\frac{7}{8} \times 25\frac{1}{8}$ in, oval
Inscr: 'Geo. Stubbs pinxit 1782'; written on the back in Stubbs' hand is the
following inscription: 'Isabella Saltonstall Aged sixteen/In the character of Una,
Spenser's Faerie Queene./From her fayre eyes he took commandment/and
ever by her looks conceived her intent'.
Prov: Miss Isabella Saltonstall; Sir William Gilbey, Bart; his executors' sale,
Christie's, 11 June, 1915 (409) bought S. Gilbey; Lt Good; Harold Good;
bought by Fitzwilliam Museum 1971.
Exh: Royal Academy, 1782 (70); Whitechapel, 1957 (13).
Lit: Mayer p. 125; Gilbey; Taylor (1, 4); Parker.
Fitzwilliam Museum, Cambridge

The subject is taken from Edmund Spenser's 'Faerie Queene' Book 1 'The
Legende of the Knight of the Red Cross or of Holinesse'. The Knight is accompanied by Una symbolizing the true religion mounted upon 'a lowly Asse more
white than snow'. Her garments are covered by 'a black stole – as one that inly
mourned' (canto 1 verse 4). Through deception he deserts her. In her search for
him Una is approached by a marauding lion (representing England). However,
he is converted by pity,

> The Lion would not leave her desolate
> But with her went along, as a strong gard
> Of her chast person and a faithfull mate
> Of her sad troubles and misfortunes hard:
> Still when she slept, he kep watch and ward,
> And when she wakt, he waited diligent,
> With humble service to he will prepard:
> From her faire eyes he took commandement
> And euer by her lookes concieved her intent

(Book 1, Canto 3, Verse 9) J. C. Smith & E. de Selincourt ed., *Spenser's Poetical
Works*, 1965.

It can be seen that Stubbs had adhered, in his iconography, extremely closely
to the written source.

Isabella Saltonstall assisted Stubbs in his last impoverished years. She was
joint executrix with Mary Spencer of Stubbs' estate. According to Joseph
Farington in his diary there existed 'a Bond of Security which gave her claim to
his pictures etc. These were sold the last week and the prices were kept up by her

agents, and many articles were bought in'.

Nollekins informed him that the sale brought in 'upwards of £4000' (in fact £4168.14.6d) but the lady had been ill-advised and bought in pictures for which high prices were bid. One in particular for which Mr Thomas Hope bid upwards of £200, yet she would not let it go'.

Miss Saltonstall had a considerable collection of Stubbs' works as an article in the *Sporting Magazine*, November 1809, shows:

It states that 'Miss Saltonstall of Cobham' was in possession of Stubbs' 'Self Portrait on horseback' a 'Horse frightened by a Lion's approach' a 'Royal Tiger' etc. No mention is made of this particular painting, but as it does not appear in the sale it seems very likely that it was in her possession.

26 *Farmer's Wife and the Raven, 1782*

Enamel on Wedgwood biscuit earthenware, $27\frac{1}{2} \times 37$ in, oval
Inscr: 'Geo. Stubbs, pinxit 1782'
Prov: Sir Walter Gilbey, Bart, his executors' sale, Christie's, 11 June 1915 (401);
Lord Tweedmouth; Lady Lever Art Gallery.
Exh: Royal Academy 1782 (120); Kenwood, 1954.
Lit: Mayer, Gilbey; Taylor (1, 3, 4); Parker.
Trustees of the Lady Lever Art Gallery, Port Sunlight

Mayer states that this work was bought by a Mrs Armstead for 100 guineas.

The subject is taken from John Gay's Fables book 1, 37. This fable is a lesson to all those who believe that disaster is caused or foretold by a conjunction of ill omens.

'That raven on yon left-hand oak
  (Curse on his ill-betiding croak)
  Bodes me no good, No more she said,
  When poor blind *Ball* with stumbling tread
  Fell prone: o'erturned the pannier lay,
  And her mash'd eggs bestrow'd the way.'
Whereas in truth:
  'Goody, the fault was all your own
  For had you laid this brittle ware
  On *Dun*, the old sure footed mare,
  Though all the ravens of the Hundred
  With croaking had your tongue out-thunder'd
  Sure footed *Dun* had kept his legs
  And you, good woman, sav'd your eggs.'
(*The Poetical Works of John Gay*, ed. G.C. Faber, Oxford University Press, 1926)

A similar engraving by Van der Gucht, from a painting by John Wootton is found in some 18th century editions of this work (Taylor, 3).

Several other versions of this subject in oils exist. It seems that Stubbs kept many of his detailed drawings (of which many examples were sold in the 1807 sale) to use again in other versions of several paintings over a considerable time. In the case of this painting one version, oil on panel is dated 1780, another 1783.

27 *Lion and Dead Tiger, 1779*

Enamel on Wedgwood biscuit earthenware, $17\frac{1}{4} \times 24$ in
Inscr: 'Geo Stubbs pinxit 1779.'
Prov: Sir Walter Gilbey, Bart; J. E. Davis; sold Christie's 16 December 1887
(54), bought Vokins; sold Christie's 12 March 1910 (154), bought Spencer;
presented by Edward P. Thompson to the Walker Art Gallery, Liverpool, 1914.
Lit: Taylor (1).
Trustees of the Walker Art Gallery, Liverpool

Lot 82 on the second day of the 1807 sale fetching £22.1.0.

It is noticeable that of the surviving works by Stubbs on Wedgwood plaques all,
save two, are of an oval format. This may be because such a shape shows up
any imperfections in the regularity of a picture far less than a rectangle. This
particular painting has a very irregular surface.

28 *Panther*

Enamel on Wedgwood biscuit earthenware, $7\frac{1}{2} \times 11$ in
Inscr: Geo: Stubbs
Prov: Not known.
Lit: Taylor (1).
Private collection

29 *Sketch for the Self-Portrait of 1781*

Pencil on paper, 12×9 in
Not inscribed
Prov: Not known
Lit: Taylor 4
Mr and Mrs Paul Mellon, Upperville, Virginia

Several drawings for the works by Stubbs on ceramic plaques are recorded in the 1807 Sale. However, none of these survive.

   This drawing has been squared up prior to its being reinterpreted and enlarged in enamel. (See B)

A *Pointer*

Enamel on copper, $9\frac{1}{2} \times 11$ in, octagonal
Inscr: 'George Stubbs pinxit 1772.'
Prov: Not known.
Exh: *Antique Dealers Fair and Exhibition*, Grosvenor House, 1955.
Lit: Taylor (1).
Private Collection

B *Self-Portrait*

Enamel on Wedgwood biscuit earthenware, 27 × 20 in, oval
Inscr: 'Geo Stubbs/pinxit 1781'; on the back, 'Geo. Stubbs painted by himself
for his friend Richd Thorold/of the Inner Temple London 1781.'
Prov: Richard Thorold; Sir John Astley; Mr and Mrs Heeley; bought at
Sotheby's, 12 July, 1967, lot 81 by National Portrait Gallery
Exh: Royal Academy, 1782 (?), '173 Portrait of an Artist'; Liverpool (27, as
Josiah Wedgwood) 1951; Whitechapel, 1957 (12).
Lit: Mayer p. 125 'Another portrait of himself, life size painted for
Mrs Thorold'; Taylor (1, 3) Parker.
Trustees of the National Portrait Gallery

The Humphry manuscript mentions this painting as being executed for Mrs
Thorold.

Until 1957 (when Mr Basil Taylor correctly identified it) it was thought to be
a portrait of Wedgwood. The preliminary drawing (See No. 29) for this portrait
uniquely demonstrates Stubbs' precise and detailed working method for these
ceramic plaques.

C *Lion attacking a Stag, 1778*

Enamel on Wedgwood biscuit earthenware, $17 \times 23\frac{1}{2}$in, oval
Inscr: 'Geo Stubbs pinxit 1778.'
Prov: Not known.
Lit: Taylor (1, 4)
Private Collection

This may be the only successful plaque of the three Wedgwood prepared in December 1778, and is possibly the 'Lion with dead Stag' lot 70 on the first day of the 1807 sale which fetched £35.14.0.

D *Stallions Fighting, 1781*

Enamel on Wedgwood biscuit earthenware, 22 × 37 in, oval
Inscr: 'Geo Stubbs pinxit 1781'
Prov: Collection of Sir Walter Gilbey, Bart; his executors' sale, Christie's,
11 June, 1915 (402).
Exh: Royal Academy, 1781 (17?); *Two Horses in Enamel*, British Institution
1806 (83).
Lit: Taylor (1, 4); Parker.
Private Collection

This appears to have been lot 96 on the second day of the 1807 sale 'Stallions
Fighting – With other Horses in a Landscape, and a Bridge in the middle dist-
ance: an oval in enamel – the spirited Action of the Animals and the splendor
of the whole stamps it an unrivaled Performance'. It fetched 160 guineas; in
1915, 17 guineas!

E *Self-Portrait on a White Hunter, 1782*

Enamel on Wedgwood biscuit earthenware, $36\frac{1}{2} \times 27\frac{1}{2}$ in, oval
Inscr: 'Geo. Stubbs pinxit 1782.'
Prov: Miss Isabella Saltonstall; Lord Tweedmouth; Lady Lever Art Gallery.
Lit: Gilbey, Taylor (1, 3, 4).
Exh: Wedgwood Bicentenary Exhibition, Hanley, 1930; Victoria and Albert
Museum, 1930 (both times as Josiah Wedgwood); Whitechapel, 1957.
Private Collection

This is presumably the 'Portrait of Mr Stubbs seated on a white hunter, an
upright oval in enamel', lot 97 on the second day of the 1807 sale, the final lot;
which was bought in by Miss Saltonstall for 290 guineas.

F   *Equestrian Portrait of Warren Hastings, 1791*

Enamel on Wedgwood biscuit earthenware, $34 \times 25\frac{1}{2}$ in, oval
Inscr: 'Geo. Stubbs pinxit 1791'
Prov: Sir Walter Gilbey, Bart; his executors' sale, Christie's, 11 June, 1915 (406).
Lit: Taylor (1, 4) Parker.
Lord Rothermere

This is presumably identical with 'the Portrait of Warren Hastings, Esq, on his celebrated Arabian, in enamel, an oval, painted in 1791' lot 68 on the second day of the 1807 sale at which it fetched £2.5.0. An exactly contemporary painting by Stubbs of the same subject was executed in oil on panel.

G *Haymakers, 1794*

Enamel on Wedgwood biscuit earthenware, $28\frac{1}{2} \times 39\frac{1}{2}$ in, oval
Inscr: 'Geo. Stubbs pinxit 1794'
Prov: Isabella Saltonstall; Sir Walter Gilbey, Bart; his executors' sale, Christie's
11 June, 1915 (394); Lady Lever Art Gallery.
Exh: British Institution, 1806 (49 or 64); Liverpool, 1951.
Lit: Taylor (1, 3, 4); Parker.
Trustees of the Lady Lever Art Gallery, Port Sunlight

This painting was lot 94 on the second day of the 1807 sale and fetched 100
guineas. A version in oil on panel is dated 1783, the mezzotint 1789.

H *Reapers, 1795*

Enamel on Wedgwood biscuit earthenware, $30\frac{1}{2} \times 41\frac{1}{2}$ in, oval
Inscr: 'Geo. Stubbs pinxit 1795'
Prov: Major A. E. W. Malcolm.
Exh: British Institution, 1806 (56); Liverpool, 1951.
Lit: Taylor; Parker.
Private Collection

Lot 93 on the second day of the 1807 sale fetching 100 gns. A version in oil on panel is dated 1783 another 1784; the mezzotint 1791.

I   *Haycarting, 1795*

Enamel on Wedgwood biscuit earthenware, $28\frac{1}{2} \times 39\frac{1}{2}$ in, oval
Inscr: 'Geo. Stubbs pinxit 1795'
Prov: Isabella Saltonstall; Sir Walter Gilbey, Bart; his executors' sale, 11 June, 1915 (395).
Exh: British Institution, 1806 (49 or 64).
Lit: Taylor (1, 3, 4); Parker.
Trustees of the Lady Lever Art Gallery, Port Sunlight

This painting was lot 69 on the second day of the 1807 sale fetching £27.6.0. Two versions in oil exist dated 1783 and 1785, the mezzotint dates from 1791.

Works in enamel by George Stubbs the whereabouts of which are unknown

From the 1807 Sale:

1st Day

Lot 47 Lion devouring a Stag – a small enamel, £1.13.0
Lot 51 Three Portraits in ovals, in enamel
Lot 64 Sleeping Tiger, in enamel, £5.5.0
Lot 66 Tiger and Tigress, in enamel – octagon, £31.10.0
Lot 71 Landscape with a Tiger in a reclining position, in enamel, £32.12.0

2nd Day

Lot 58 A Lion, in oval enamel
Lot 78 Lions, in enamel, a pair, ovals, £6.16.6
Lot 83 Head of an Old Man, a small oval, in fine enamel on copper, and a ditto, a small upright, in enamel, £5.5.0
Lot 84 Lion & Lioness, in square enamel, accomplished with great Spirit and Truth, £31.10.0
Lot 85 Portrait of a Lion seated on a Rock in enamel, £21.0.0
Lot 91 Horse affrighted at a Lion, finely expressive of terror at the Lion's approach, highly finished in enamel on copper

From Mayer – Memoirs of Thomas Dodd, William Upcott and George Stubbs R.A., Liverpool 1879:

Copy of the 'Bricklayers' (Labourers) for Dr Erasmus Darwin

Portrait of a Youth, William Shafto Esq.
A small rough lap dog, the size of life, painted for Mrs French

Portrait of Dr Hardy M.D. (For Mrs Thorold)

From the catalogue of Old Wedgwood at the Liverpool Exhibition of 1879:

'1475 A PLAQUE, probably in white jasper ware, on which is painted, in enamel, a landscape, with recumbent figure of a lion. Signed by George Stubbs, the eminent animal painter, for whom Wedgwood states (see Reprint of "Wedgwood's Catalogue" p. 97) that he made special tablets.'

In the possession of Mr Stamford, 1905:

Lion and Tiger Fighting
Horse and Lion Fighting
each 'size about 24 × 18 ins. oval'

Letters

Throughout this catalogue considerable reference has been made to the letters of Josiah Wedgwood to Thomas Bentley in which frequent mention is made of Stubbs. As these letters present the only surviving account of the artist's working methods apart from the unpublished Humphry manuscript they are reproduced verbatim.

The first mention of Stubbs is not about the plaques, but concerns the proposal to make palettes for his Queen's Ware.

From Wedgwood, Etruria, to Bentley, Greek Street, Soho, London, 18 October 1777. (E25.18785)

I am afraid Mr. Stubs will find our pallet of Queens Ware too heavy for his hand. We had a specimen of a light earth some time since from the late D. of Athol which might be very useful upon this, & other occasions if we could have a few hundreds weight. Can you make any enquiries after it, by letter or otherwise?

A meeting with the artist and Bentley seems to have spurred Wedgwood into action.

From Wedgwood to Bentley, 4 November 1777. (E25.18791)

My comp.ts to Mr. Stubbs. He shall be gratified but large Tablets are not the work of a day – We have been labouring at the apparatus for that purpose from the day I came down, & can report – *some progress*

From Wedgwood, Etruria, to Bentley, Turnham Green, near London, 26 November 1777. (E25.18797)

One or two of Mr. Stubb's tablets go into the kiln on Thursday next, but they are not large,

abo.t 22 by 17. We are preparing larger but must proceed by gentle degree.

From Wedgwood, Etruria, to Bentley, Turnham Green, near London, 11 December 1777. (E25.18800)

P.S. We have fired 3 tablets at different times for Mr. Stubs, one of which is perfect, the other two are crack'd & broke all to pieces. We shall send the whole one (22 inches by 17) on Saturday & are preparing some larger.

There is now a gap of nearly a year and Wedgwood is still trying to perfect the plaques.

From Wedgwood, Etruria, to Bentley at Richard L. Edgeworth, North Church, near Great Berkhamstead, Herts, 17 October 1778. (E26.18856)

When you see Mr. Stubs pray tell him how hard I have been labouring to furnish him with the means of adding immortality to his very excellent pencil. I mean only to arrogate to myself the honor of being his *canvas maker*. But alass this honor is at present denied to my endeavors, though you may assure him that I will succeed if I live a while longer undisturbed by the french as I only want an inclin'd plane that will stand our fire. My first attempt has failed, & I cannot well proceed in my experiments 'till we lay by work for xmas when our kilns will be at liberty for my trials.

The letter of 30 May 1779 contains the first mention of Stubbs executing the Family Portrait and other work for Wedgwood.

From Wedgwood, Etruria, to Bentley, 30 May 1779. (E26.18894)

I wrote to you by post this morning, but wish to

say a word or two concerning Mr. Stubbs & his tablets.

We shall be able now to make them with certainty & success of the size of the 3 in this inv? & I hope soon to say as far as 30 inches, – perhaps ultimately up to 36 inches by 24, but that is at present in the offing & I wo.^d not mention to Mr. Stubbs beyond 30 at present. If Mr. Stubbs succeeds he will be followed by others to which he does not seem to have the least objection, but rather wishes for it; & if the oil painters too should use them they may become a considerable object.

At present I think we should give Mr. Stubbs every encouragement to proceed & establish the fashion. He wishes you know to do something for us by way setting off against the tablets. My picture, & Mrs. Wedgwoods in enamel will do something. Perhaps he may take your governess & you in by the same means. I should have no objection to a family piece, or rather two, perhaps, in oil, if he sho.^d visit us this summer at Etruria. These things will go much beyond his present trifling debt to us.

Now I wish you to see Mr. Stubbs, & if the idea meets your approbation, to tell him that if it is convenient for him to pay in money for what he has hitherto had, it will pay something towards the kilns, & alterations in kilns we have made, & other expenses we have been at in our essays, & the next £100 or £150 in tablets, perhaps more, shall be work & work – we will take the payment in paintings.
The two family pieces I have hinted at above I mean to contain the children only, & grouped perhaps in some such manner as this.

Sukey playing upon her harpsichord, with Kitty singing to her which she often does, & Sally & Mary Ann upon the carpet in some employment suitable to their ages. This to be one picture. The pendant to be Jack standing at a table making fixable air with the glass apparatus

&c., & his two brothers accompanying him. Tom jumping up & clapping his hands in joy & surprise at seeing the stream of bubbles rise up just as Jack has put a little chalk to the acid. Joss with the chemical dictionary before him in a thoughtful mood, which actions will be exactly descriptive of their respective characters.

My first thought was to put these two pictures into Mr. Wright's hands; but other ideas took place, & remembering the labourers, & cart in the exhibition, with paying for tablets &c. I ultimately determin'd in favor of Mr. Stubbs, & have mention'd a fire piece to Mr. Wright in a letter I wrote him the last week to tell him I should be glad to see him here in a fortnight or 3 weeks. But what shall I do about having Mr. S. & Mr. W. here at the same time, will they draw kindly together think you. Once more farewell.

Again there is a gap until the letter of 7 August 1780 by which time Stubbs is at Etruria.

From Wedgwood, Etruria, to Bentley, Turnham Green, near London, 7 August 1780. (L.H.P.)

We have been considering & reconsidering some subjects besides tablets for Mr. Stubs to paint in enamel, & are now making some large jarrs for that purpose. The present idea is to cover them over with painting, with ground figures, trees & sky without any borderes or divisons, in short to consider the whole surface as one piece of canvas & cover it accordingly, & under this idea we find a simple jarr form the best for our purpose, & they will come cheap enough which, as times are, may be something in their favor.

This morning we are going for the second time to the works to see the jarrs turned & to prepare some clay tablets for modeling upon, & we shall then dine with the good parson of Newcastle so that this day is fully provided for only we must find time for a lecture upon perspective which science Mr. Stubs has kindly engaged to teach my boys.

Mr. Stubs, it seems, has been a drawing master amongst other things, at Heath's Academy, though he followed that profession but a short time. He begun by teaching perspective to his pupils, which he believes to be just as rational a method in draw^g, as learning the letters first is acquiring the art of reading, & he would have the learner to copy nature & not drawings.

From Wedgwood, Etruria, to Bentley, 13 August 1780. (L.H.P.)

Just before your last came to hand, not many minutes before, I was telling Mr. Stubs that our vases would sell if they were painted with free masterly sketches in which way they might be got out of hand, but that our stippleing method was tedious beyond all bearing. He was of the same opinion, & will try his hand upon half a doz^n jarrs we have made for that purpose, but these are only for himself & friends, & I have not made any other proposals to him – perhaps it will be best to defer it till he has tried his hand upon his jarrs.

We make but little progress with the family piece at present, but Mr. S. talks of laying to in good earnest soon. He has fixed upon his subject for modeling, *the lion & horse* from his own engraving. He objected to every other subject so I gave it up, & he is now laying in the horse whilst I am writing a few letters this good Sunday morning. He does very well so far, & with a little practice will probably be as much master of his modeling tools, as he is of his pencils. I will write you farther as we proceed.

Our three little lassies & their coach are just put into colors & the characters of the children are hit off very well. I have given him one sitting, & this is all we have done with the picture. The stable is preparing, & the horses are

to *sit* this week.

We are still open to the sky in our kitchen, which, though the weather is fine as could be wished for, is nevertheless an uncomfortable situation for animals whose nature urges them to go through the drudgery of eating three or four times a day – Oh! for the sleep of a Dormouse, or the life of a Toad in a stone for a few weeks till our troubles are past & we safely cover'd in from the wind, & open air again.

For people in such a situation we are all pretty well thank you. Mr. Stubs's ambitious tooth which had started up at least 1/8 of an inch above its level is fallen to its level again & permits him to eat his bread in peace.

Susans tooth is better, but not well; she sends her love & thanks for your kind enquiries. All here unite in love & best compliments to your good lady & self.

From Wedgwood, Etruria, to Bentley, 21 August 1780. (L.H.P.)

On Monday last I took Mr. Stubs to Trentham to look at the fine views there. Ld Gower was polite enough to ride with us thro' the park & grounds & shew us their beauties, but there was too much variety to fix a single sketch upon paper though that was Mr. Stubs's original design. This morning was spent in mere viewing of the finest scenes, Mr. S. says, he ever saw, & the remainder of the day in feasting the body & mind in his L^{d}ships mansion. We would have excused ourselves from dining out of mere covetousness of time as Mr. S. lamented his having done so little since he came here. But his L^{d}ship would not be denied, and what could we little folks do but submit to the will of the L^d S^r. Wm. Gordon & his Lady. Lady--- a daughter of Ld Dunmores with Lady Louisa McDonald, & their own family made up the company. We had a great deal of conversation &

chat upon various subjects but not a single word upon politics. They are not talk'd at Trentham this season.

Tuesday & Wednesday Mr. Stubs modeled & painted a little, & on Thursday and Friday nearly finished his tablet whilst I was at Stafford making peace between Mr. Adderley & Mr. Sparrow, which I happily effected in two days negotiation without bringing their matters into court, & I believe very much to both their satisfactions. Mr. Adderleys mother came from London to have been an evidence & was very happy in being disappointed. She enquir'd after Mrs. Bentley & you.

Mr. S. has now quite finished his tablet & we will send you a copy very soon either in blue & white, or to save time, in one color.

Our picture proceeds very slowly, but we have begun to make the horses *sit* this morning, & I write this by Mr. Stubs in the new stable, which is to be my study whilst he is painting there.

From Wedgwood to Bentley, 9 September 1780. (L.H.P.)

Our picture, & building go on pretty currently, but neither one nor the other approach towards a finish. Mr. Stubs dines with Mr. Swinnerton tomorrow, & is to paint the old gentleman when he has done with me. We dine with S.ᵗ Thomas Broughton the next week & I apprehend will have something to do there. Mr. FitsWilliams has asked his prices & he has money enough now. We have dined, & shall dine with all the gentlemen in the country & I hope Mr. S will be benefited by the addition he will make here to his acquaintance.

From Wedgwood, Etruria, to Bentley, 14 September 1780. (L.H.P.)

Mr. Stubs is gone to Mr. Swinnertons today for the week out. Our picture goes on very slowly, but we may report *some progress* & I think the likeness promise to be strong, but I do not know what to say upon this subject because the likenesses in those that approach towards being finished grows weaker as the painting increases. Mr Stubs says the likeness will come in & go off many times before finishing so I can say nothing to this matter at present, only that the first sketches were very strong likenesses, & the after touches have hitherto made them less so, but I daresay he will bring them about again before he takes his final leave of the picture.

From Wedgwood, Stone, to Bentley, Turnham Green, near London, 25 September 1780. (L.H.P.)

Mr. Stubbs came to us again last night after finishing a portrait of Mr. Swinnerton which is much admired, & I think deservedly so by all who have seen it, & I hope this, with our family picture & some others which he will probably paint before he leaves us will give him a character which will be entirely new to him here, for nobody suspects Mr. Stubs of painting anything but horses & lions, or dogs & tigers, & I can scarcely make anybody believe that he ever attempted a human figure.

I find Mr. S. repents much his having established this character for himself. I mean that of horse painter, & wishes to be considered as an history, & portrait painter. How far he will succeed in bringing about the change at his time of life I do not know. The exhibition may do wonders for him.

From Wedgwood, Etruria, to Bentley, Turnham Green, near London, 8 October 1780. (L.H.P.)

As I am leaving home this morning for a day or two upon a visit to Cotton, which is to be return'd on Tuesday by water, I must just tell my dear friend that we are all alive & well & proceed, though slowly with our works of the pencil & trowil, & Mr. Stubs now talks of finishing in a fortnight. Besides the family piece he has made some progress in a portrait of my father which will be a very strong likeness. What may turn up for him in other places we do not yet know. His pieces I rather apprehend are beyond the limited conceptions of this country. He has been applied to by S^r. T. Broughton for his price of painting a horse, & by another for a dog, but we have heard no farther from either. Two family pieces have been a little talked of, but it is natural to suppose they will wait to see the specimen in hand finished before they determine upon anything.

From Wedgwood, Etruria, to Bentley, Turnham Green, near London, 21 October 1780. (L.H.P.)

Mr. Stubs is now drawing to a conclusion & talks of going to Liverpool in a few days; but I think he is not quite so near a finish as he seems to apprehend. He thinks he has finish'd six of the children, the horses & little carriage. The children are most of them strong, but not very delicate likenesses – Some parts are either a little caricatur'd, or my own eyes & those of many of my friends are much deciev'd. He certainly has not observ'd Mrs. Montagu's maxim respecting her model, but I will not say any more upon this subject at present, *& this is only to yourself,* as it would be hardly fair 'till the picture is turned out of his hands as completely finished, & besides he has promised me to compare the originals & copies carefully together & give any last touches

which may be found wanting as soon as he has brought my wife, my daughter Susan & my-self up with the rest. I think he has not been so happy in hitting off the likenesses of the two former as he has in the others. I have been sitting a great of the day, but cannot report much progress.

Time & patience in large doses, are absolutely necessary in these cases & methinks I would not be a portrait painter upon any condition whatever. We are all heartily tired of the business, & I think the painter has more reason than any of us to be so.

From Wedgwood, Etruria, to Bentley, 28 October 1780. (L.H.P.)

Mr. Stubs has just now begun upon a picture as large as that he has painted for me – It is Mr. & Mrs. Fitzwilliams at breakfast as large as life, & he will probably have more to do before he leaves us. He sleeps with us & wishes to employ some of his evenings in modeling a companion to his frighten'd horse, & has fixed upon one of his Phaetons for that purpose, but cannot proceed till he has the print of this subject which he says may be had at some of the print shops, but he does not know which. There are two prints of Phaetons, in that which he would have the two *nearest* horses are fighting, & in that which he would not have the middlemost, or farthest are fighting. He desires Mr. Brock will find him this print & send it down by the first coach that he may have time to complete the model whilst he stays here.

I have objected to this subject as a companion to the frightened horse as that is a piece of natural history, this is a piece of un-natural fiction, & indeed I should prefer something less hackney'd & shall still endeavour to convert him, but would nevertheless wish to have the Phaeton sent lest he should be obstinate in which case I think it will be better to have that than nothing.

Mr. Stubs is likewise very desirous of seeing my picture framed & wishes me to write for one today to be sent down as soon as possible, but it will not do to write to a frame maker to send a frame of such & such dimensions; I must trouble my dear friend to look in Leicester Square or at some other frame makers & chuse a pattern for me. It must be $5^{ft}-11\frac{1}{2}^{ins}$ by $3-11\frac{1}{2}$ within & not less than 6 or 7 inches broad. Mr. FitzWilliams will wait till he sees mine & if he likes it will order another of the same. I have put down my idea of a section on the other side, but it is not meant to bind your choice for ten to one I should alter mine if I saw a variety, & as you know the subject of the picture I leave the choice entirely to your good taste, Mrs. Bentley being of the council. I have only to mention farther that we would have the frame come down in such a case as will serve to bring up the picture to the exhibition, the top to be screwed & not nailed on. Another frame is wanted for my fathers head $2^{ft}-3\frac{1}{2}^{in}$ by $1-11\frac{1}{4}$ on the inside which should be of a grave cast suitable to the age of the subject.

Mr. Stubs thinks he has quite finish'd our picture, but he is a little mistaken for I shall get him to make a few alterations still but it must be by degrees, for I have plagued him a good deal in the last finishing strokes & he has been very good in bearing with my impertinence.

From Wedgwood, Etruria, to Bentley,
12 November 1780. (L.H.P.)

Mr. Stubbs is still at Mr. FitzWilliams's, only he sleeps here, but Mr. F.W^s is now in town, & I intend to take the opportunity of his absence to prevail upon Mr. S. to give us another day or two at our family piece which does not appear to me to be quite finish'd. My wife I think very deficient – Mary Ann more so, & Susan is not hit off well at all. I say nothing of myself, but upon the whole agree with Mr. Edgeworth that there is much to praise, & a little to blame. As soon as *I think* the picture finish'd I will hie away to kiss your hand at Turnham Green.

The model of Phaeton is in some forwardness – He works hard at it every night almost 'till bedtime.

Addenda

A bill exists in the Wedgwood archives (E22. 10166) from the Greek Street premises to Etruria. It appears that originally Stubbs' account was entered in the books of the Wedgwood and Bentley partnership. However, after the death of Bentley the account seems to have been taken on personally by Wedgwood at least as far as the years 1778 and 1781 are concerned:

Mr. Stubbs Dr.
1778 To Wedgwood and Bentley
28 Nov.ʳ To Tablets   27. 6.0
30 Dec.ʳ —do—   1. 4.9
1779
25 Feby —do—   7.18.0
 7 Feby —do—   27. 2.0
                       ————
                      63.10.9

As I presume Mr. W. means to take this account upon himself Mr. Swift will please to settle it between the Co. and him and let T.B. know that he may close the Account.

1781
10 Oct.ʳ Mr. Stubbs to J.W. Tablets 23.1.0

These are charged to Mr. W, in the Co's Sales – but T.B. believes they were made by Mr. Wedgwood – He does not know whether this mode is perfectly right or not – Mr. Swift will be so good as examine whether they are charged to debit of Co's Stock –
    I take it for granted that the Inv.º to Mr. Stubbs of the 20th Jany 1781 which you lately sent up is all the account which you have against him.

The 1787 Wedgwood catalogue includes the following excerpt under Class XVII which demonstrates that Wedgwood hoped to extract some publicity value out of the relationship.

TABLETS, for chimneypieces, for cabinets, and for inlaying, are enriched with the same species of painting. These tablets are, from the bracelet size, to 18 or 20 inches diameter. Some have been made, for that excellent artist Mr. Stubbs, so large as 36 inches, and his exquisite enamels upon them after nature, which have been repeatedly exhibited in the Royal Academy, are evidences of the species and value of the enamel paintings that may be produced upon these tablets.

In view of this it is somewhat surprising that Stubbs did not emphasize the Wedgwood connection.

The following passage is, in relation to Stubbs' work in enamel colours, the most significant part of the biographical notes composed by Ozias Humphry, the various MS versions of which are in the Picton Library, Liverpool. Like much else in this entire document the text has to be treated somewhat reservedly as there are significant points at which it conflicts plainly with the evidence afforded by the painter's work, but a critical examination of these differences of account or interpretation lies outside the scope of the present catalogue.   B. Taylor

About the year 1771 he determined to make experiments & improvements in enamel painting. Mr Cosway had received some commissions to paint loose and amorous subjects from abroad, and in discoursing together, it was this artist who first suggested to him the idea of attempting subjects in this line of Enamel: upon which, after having considered the matter he willingly acquiesced, if it were possible to find a Tablet of the size of a Quarter of a sheet of post paper. This was one condition; and the other was if it were practicable to produce Colours to work with of the appearance they were required to be when the pictures were fired. For this purpose he set about to make himself a complete sett of Colours on a new principle; and after a series of attempts with various success which continued the space of two years with great expense & endless labour & study, generally making written memorandums of his experiments. He at length completed a sett, having out of more than 100 lbs weight of colour produced about 81 lbs some ounces fit for his purpose –, making in all nineteen different tints, but after the Colours were prepared & in order it was near three years before the large plates which he had been promised him were rendered so perfect as to be fit for use; in the mean time he painted upon the largest copper plates he could find. – It should be noticed that these experiments, as his engravings had formerly been at leisure days and hours between the Commissions he held and was executing, never laying any task aside, by which it must appear from the time that was required to do them that his general business for oil pictures was beginning to fail him.–

Enamel plates upon Copper of the size of 12 Inches diameter & of 18 by 15 inches, were without further difficulty procured and were accordingly used by him for various subjects, and these seem the largest plates that could possibly be made upon Copper: but their dimensions not reaching the wishes and conceptions of Mr Stubbs, he made application to the Potteries and the Artificial Stone manufacturers; the latter of whom not willing to undertake the Commission, Messrs Wegwood and Bentley engaged in it and in 1778 actually produced plates of their ware of the sizes of Three feet six or seven inches wide, by two feet six or seven Inches high, plates of a stupendous dimension compared with what had been commonly used for enamel painting. – Having thus prepared himself he went on with his professional practice alternating painting in oil Colours & Enamel as were offered to him, or during the the intervals of public employment as his humour inclined him. –

Lenders

Trustees of the British Museum 17, 21

Fitzwilliam Museum, Cambridge 25

Trustees of the Lady Lever Art Gallery,
Port Sunlight 18, 26

Trustees of the National Portrait Gallery,
London 24

Mr and Mrs Paul Mellon 29

Private Collections 8, 11, 20, 24, 28

Royal Academy of Arts 1, 2

Tate Gallery 3, 6, 15

Victoria and Albert Museum 7

Walker Art Gallery, Liverpool 26

Trustees of the Wedgwood Museum, Barlaston
4, 4a, 9, 10, 12, 13, 14, 19, 22, 23a, b, c